# Explore the Inner Universe

HANSRAJ HARITASH

The creator has blessed everyone with infinite power. Everyone is a beautiful expression of the creation. We all are witnesses to experience the creation on behalf of the creator who is residing inside us. This book is an attempt to reinvent ourselves to get a broader perspective of our real self, our life, our world, and our universe. It is just like adding more cameras at different angles to get a 360-degree view in the game of life to broaden the perspective of the player about the self, others, and the game itself. Our choices define our role in the play of life. Our choices are a mirror reflecting our character. If our choices are beautiful, so too will we be. It's simple. Life is all about choices, from how we treat ourselves to how we face our battles, which are reflected in how we treat others. Every experience in life makes us either bitter or better, depending on the choices we opt for. Let the positive choices sculpt us into a masterpiece. Opt for kindness, bravery, and authenticity and radiate it to become a source of it. Choose wisely, live beautifully and keep testing the inner limits to become the best version of self. In the end, we all are stories and being the actors, it is our sole responsibility to play it well and make our story the best!!

"YOU ARE ABSOLUTELY CAPABLE OF CREATING THE LIFE YOU CAN'T STOP THINKING ABOUT."
—THE UNIVERSE

# Contents

# 01

# Our Infinite Power

The universe is everything. It includes all of space, and all the matter and energy that space contains. It includes the earth, the moon and all planets and their many dozens of moons along with asteroids and comets which orbit the Sun in the Milky Way galaxy. There are hundreds of billions of stars and billions of galaxies in the universe. All the stars in all the galaxies and all the other stuff that astronomers can't even observe are all part of the universe. It includes all of us and time itself. It is, simply, everything.

The quest to unravel the mysteries of the universe has captivated human minds for centuries. Then the question arises: how does everything work in order, and who is running the infinite universe? There must be something, as everything cannot come from nothing, and even if it comes out of nothing, the perseverance is not possible without the guiding/controlling power. In all religions, the Supreme power is believed to be the cause of all things and so is seen as the creator, sustainer, and ruler of the universe.

The so-called Supreme power is actively involved in the running of the universe. It set our universe in motion and inaugurated a divine unfolding plan, a progressive evolutionary design. It preserves, holds, and sustains everything, which ranges from the universe itself to the smallest particle on the planet.

All forces work through the law of nature. Consequently, the Supreme power is not aloof from his creation. Everything is alive, unfolding, and continually involved in the ongoing systems of creation.

A lot of ancient philosophies around the globe classify the composition of the universe into five elements: Earth, Water, Fire, Air and Ether (Space). These are also called the "Panch Mahabhoot". Each elements represents a state of matter in nature. Solid matter is classified as the "earth" element. Water is everything that is liquid. Air is everything that is a gas. Fire is that part of nature that transforms one state of matter into another. Space is the mother of the other elements. All natural things are connected with the creator through these basic elements of life. These "Panch Mahabhoot" the fundamental constituents of the universe, and their balance is crucial for exploring the infinite power of the universe.

We nourish ourselves with foods that come from the earth, and eventually, our body returns to the earthly matter from which it came. Fire provides the body with heat and radiant energy. Water is our life-sustaining liquid, making up more than 70 percent of our total body mass. Air gives movement to biological functions and feeds every cell with oxygen. Space provides the other elements with an opportunity to interact in the different possible ways.

The five elements explain why substances of the natural world are harmonious with the human body. It is only through these elements that the Supreme power has established a relationship with all of us.

The Supreme power constitutes an ecosystem wherein humans, plants, animals, and other organisms, as well as weather and landscapes, come together to form a bubble of life. These basic elements of life are the connection between everything on the earth, which strings everyone together. We, as human beings, have the power of thinking apart from five elements which differentiate us. With the help of reasoning and insight, we can understand these five elements, the laws of nature, and the creator itself. The basic understanding of these five elements helps us to stay in balance physically, mentally, spiritually, and emotionally. It played a crucial role in our understanding of our body, our thinking, our cosmos and the creation of the creator.

At the substance level, all the natural things are made of the same components/material. These elements are the building blocks of all material existence. Our consciousness introduces us to a conscious creative force that wants to be known and leaves tools and traces by which we can discover that creator. Evolution itself is one such trace, and it assembles everything to accomplish that end. We can experience the creator and its workings around us.

The cosmic consciousness of our soul makes the whole universe our family, and we find that the creator, the universe, and we are the same. The creator uses our consciousness to manifest and experience the creation. The universe is the sum total of all the creations, and all are unified under the creator. We are not separate from the creator. We have a divine consciousness and are blessed with the soul to experience, the mind to think, the sense to feel, and the body to express. The divine consciousness aligns ourselves with the cosmic consciousness through which we feel the presence of God in every particle. This consciousness takes us closer to the broader perspective of the creator and gives us a sense of belonging with all the creation of the creator.

It is the only way to experience the creator. When we start experiencing the creator, we feel that the creator is not a person but rather an energy with cosmic consciousness and the intelligence of the universe. If we observe the consciousness of the smallest particle of the universe, we will experience the intelligence of the Supreme energy which makes it happen.

The intelligence which creates and preserves the universe is omnipotent, omniscient, and omnipresent. Our cosmic consciousness reflects the God who created it with the majestic purpose of eternal life. It makes us an infinite energy hub.

Everything uses the energy that comes from the universe and powers the universe in return, as energy is neither created nor destroyed. It can only be changed from one form to another. The transformation of energy depends on our interactions with each other in the ecosystem. The ecosystem functions through energy transfer mechanisms on which every living thing depends. Our thoughts and feelings are energy as well, so everything we think and feel has an influence on everything and everyone in this universe. We need to be aware of the infinite power of the universe as the same energy resides inside us to experience the feast of earth called life.

The same was mentioned in the Brihadaranyaka Upanishad, which defines the concept "Aham Brahmasmi". It unites the macrocosmic ideas of God and universal consciousness with the microcosmic individual expression of the Self. This mantra highlights the notion that all beings are intimately connected to universal energy and cannot be separated from it. To recite Aham Brahmasmi is to recognise that Brahman and Atman are one, and as such, there can be no ego or sense of separation. We have infinite power because of the God particle within ourselves, and that God particle belongs to the universe.

We are the sources of infinite power, have everything within ourselves, and it is reflected everywhere in the form of energy in the universe. The awareness comes with knowing the creator and the real self. The more precisely we know the inner self, the more accurately we get connected with the creator and its infinite power to create our own destiny.

# 02

# Know the Self

Once we understand the cosmic power which sustains everything, then the question comes about the identity of ourselves. We are all well aware of our physical body and the role, position, and relation acquired by the body. But all this is what we acquired. To know the real self, we have to go deeper where we find that we are much more than the body, and the body is just the instrument for the manifestation of energy.

We are all an aura or energy or electromagnetic field surrounded by a physical body. Our body is a source of magnetic fields. The sun is electric and builds our DNA. The earth is magnetic and holds the entire universe for us. The moon empowers the consciousness. The trees absorb the negative energy of the planet. The oceans make life possible on the earth. We get energy from the universe and return the energy back to the universe in a particular pattern. The more we are aware of ourselves, our aura, our electric field, the higher the connection with the creator which makes all arrangements for us. The curiosity of awareness starts with the question, who am I?

The worthiness of the question, the uniqueness of the question and the beauty of the question is that the answer varies from person to person. Moreover, the outsider can share the experience, which will act just like knowledge/information, but the real beauty lies in experiencing the answer. The answer is already given everywhere in Veda, Upanishad, Bhagavad Gita, Bible, Quran and all other religious scriptures, which simply explain that we are the soul, but the answer cannot be understood in the true sense if the curiosity of the question does not arise within. This question is not a basic question; rather, this question is the beginning of discovering the inner universe.

We perceive our surroundings, environment, and the world around us through our sense organs, which receive and convey sensory information to the brain. I see the world through my eyes but perceive everything within myself. I hear outside noise but actually hear it inside me. I smell things outside, but the sensation goes within me. I taste different outside food items through my tongue, but the taste experienced inside me. I touch anything outside, but the sensation is felt inside. We consider that everything is happening outside but the reality is everything is going on inside. All this happens because the experiencer inside us experiences the energy field. It is because of something inside that the outside world exists for us. So, I decided to go inside to know the answer.

When I found it difficult to unlayer myself, I decided to sort out what I am not, as after that process, whatever is left in me will probably actually be me. I realised that I am not the body, not the mind, not the emotions, not the senses, not the habits/actions because I exist even if some of my body part is taken apart, even if my habits change, even if I lose my memory. I am not even the content of consciousness as

I am present even when I am unconscious in my deep sleep. I am not the breath as it's not mine; I don't take breath, it just comes itself. Then only the experiencer left in me who is connected to my body through the consciousness of the soul.

I have been seeing myself for the first time even when I have not even developed basic knowledge. I have seen my body transforming from a kid to an adult. I have gained knowledge and experiences in the journey of life. So, I am not just the knowledge and experiences; rather, I am the experiencer. I experience all the changes that go through my body, mind, thoughts, and emotions in a conscious, subconscious, and unconscious state of mind. The experiencer inside us doesn't even have its separate consciousness; rather, it has the cosmic consciousness, which connects us with the entire cosmos. We may be different at the level of appearance, but at the level of substance, we all are the same. We all are the one.

We can understand ourselves at three different levels, i.e. body, mind and soul. The body is created by the creator with five basic elements of life, that is Panch Mahabhoot and blessed with the sense organs to perceive the universe through the mind, with 3 Gunas (qualities) to act or react and to accept or reject thoughts and manifest the thoughts into reality. The soul, which is the experiencer, experiences the world through the consciousness of the mind and perception of the body.

For a better understanding of the self at the level of the body, we have to understand the "Panchtatva", i.e. the five elements of life. The entire life system is based on the harmonious functioning of these basic elements. The more we are connected with the Panchtatva, the closer we are to our real self to experience the experiencer or Supreme energy of the universe which resides inside our body. The creator has blessed us with a body made of the God particle, but the "Panchtatva" within ourselves belongs to the universe.

We should have a sense of submission to the creator for a blessed body. The Bhagavad Gita says that the best way of submission at the level of the body is through karma. Karma, which serves the existence of all living things, is the best return gift to the creator. This is the real Prasad to distribute. If we have submission to the creator, we are automatically submitting all our anxieties and fears related to the body and our existence to the creator. It helps us to focus only on our karma.

At the level of the body, we are the karmayogi whose every cell of the body should manifest the infinite energy of the universe with the finite body, respecting the law of nature and giving the best experiences to the creator residing within me.

At the level of the mind, we have the sense organs through which all pleasure and pains are perceived. According to Hinduism, the mind has three Gunas (qualities): Rajogun (Rajas) Brahma, Satogun (Sattva) Vishnu, and Tamogun (Tamas) Shiv. These qualities give birth to thoughts. Our thought and thinking made our perception and we manifest our thinking into reality in the universe through our perception. We have to be just aware about ourselves. If we're not aware of our own thoughts, aware of our own thoughts, they will eventually turn into habits, routines, impulses, and reactions, then start controlling us.

We have to remember that we are the owners of our minds, and we have power beyond what the mind can think, as we are infinite. The unique thing about reasoning and insight is that the moment we start feeling we have enough knowledge, we would close the door to life. We are much more than our thoughts. This awareness will take down the curtains of the mind and streamline our thinking.

The love and compassion for the creation of the creator help us to streamline our thinking in constructive ways.

The universe responds to our thoughts and feelings. Our vibrations are connected to the Supreme energy of the universe. When we align ourselves with the flow of the universe, we feel the same energy and infiniteness inside ourselves.

We witness the world only through the perception of sense organs. In deep sleep, when there is no perception, no thought, no memory, there is no observer too. There is no separation between the observer and the observation. The real purpose is to clear the mind to see beyond the mind and know the inner self. It is not suppressing of thoughts; rather, it is to see beyond the thoughts. Once we clear the dust of mind which is God's abode, we find the God residing within us.

At the level of the soul, there is oneness. We all are the same. Cosmic consciousness is a perfect awareness of the oneness of life. The universe is filled with one life, and the whole universe is ours. We all are bubbles made of the same water. We all are sculptures made of the same soil. We all are the different reflections of the same light.

If we experience the knowledge of self thoroughly, we come to know there is no separate self at all. I am at the level of body made of Panchtatva, which belongs to the universe. I am at the level of mind having senses and consciousness. We humans have a unique capacity for language and thinking to connect with cosmic consciousness. I am at the level of soul; we are exactly the same as the creator and have a sense of oneness with everything. It is just the blessing of the universe that the life manifested within myself. We should have gratitude and submission to creation for the favour.

The best answer about the real self will come automatically when we start to see ourselves as it is. Even we don't need an answer. If we keep starting to ask questions, we will find the answer in form of submission to the creator for every answer, devotion to the creator, love and compassion for the creations of the creator which will help in streamlining of thinking and turning our consciousness into a cosmic consciousness. At this stage, we realise that we are part of the Supreme energy. The creator has blessed us with a human body, mind for reasoning and insight with cosmic consciousness. Our energy affects the entire universe through our karma, thinking and consciousness. We are all, in effect, miniature universes. Each personal life and experience is a micro- universe.

# 03

# Purpose of Existence

The questions which often arise in my mind are why we exist and what our destiny is. What is the purpose of our existence? Why are we here? Even if we believe that we are born by chance, is there nothing else to it? If we want to find a genuine answer to this question, we must be mindful of the world around us and of all things that exist here and learn from our observation the interdependence and interrelatedness of the whole existence, which are at the crux of it. Everything in creation is directly or indirectly connected to the rest of creation, just like the spokes in a wheel. We are not alone here, and we cannot live alone. Our actions affect others, just as theirs affect us.

Let's start with the basics. All life forms share at least one essential purpose, which is survival. The survival of the fittest theory suggests that the organisms best adapted to the environment are more likely to survive. Once we ensure survival, we engage in pleasures and comforts to attain peace and happiness. When we find that pleasure and comforts are not the absolute tools to attain peace and happiness, we move towards the spiritual path to search for the purpose of existence.

The German philosopher Kierkegaard explained it very beautifully by dividing spheres of existence into three distinguished stages: the aesthetic, the ethical, and the religious. Each of these "stages on life's way" represents competing views on life and potentially conflicts with one another. At the beginning of life, we blindly run after our desires and pleasures. It attracts us for some time, but the moment we come out of it, we feel it is not everything, and we start thinking beyond all these. We slowly move towards an ethical life. After a time, we get fed up with this and move towards spiritual life. The height of materialism is the beginning of the spiritualism. The same is explained by a shayari in a beautiful way "फितूर होता है हर उम्र में जुदा जुदा , खिलौना, माशुका और फिर ख़ुदा"

Till the time we are in the aesthetic or ethical stage of life, we are so busy in the outside world that we don't even have the time to think about the internal universe and the purpose of existence. It is spirituality which teaches us to go inside. When we go deep inside, we get a different answer and perspective on the purpose of existence. The answer is very subjective whereas our conscious mind has objective knowledge only. The conscious mind is not broad enough to answer this subjective question. Let's try to get an answer from the conscious mind by making the question objective and making a list of why we have not come to the earth. This might be answered by the conscious mind. We all know we have not come here to take trouble, to give trouble, or to live in pain. First of all, start working on the entire list for which we have not come here; eventually, we find that we are left with the answer.

Sometimes, we search the purpose of life out of pain. Let's understand the answer when we are in pain. It starts with the question: When the Supreme power is so powerful, why it had not created a perfect life to live in, and a perfect relationship in everyone's life? Why things are not so perfect? Why do we all know and experience pain, sickness, and hurt? Why can we all even think of evil? What would be the purpose of pain and suffering in anyone's life? Who is creating that pain, and what is the intention behind it? We have to understand that the creator need not be required to select us (1 out of 10 lakh sperm) as humans and 1 out of 84 lakh species on the earth and 1 out of billions of galaxies and created the entire cosmos just to punish us. The thinking of the creator can never be so destructive.

God has not created pain; it is the desire for pleasure which brings the pain, as pleasure and pain are the two sides of the same coin. We have pain and suffering because we may have chosen them unintentionally. We have hundreds of reasons to smile, but we hold onto that one reason for pain so tightly that we unwittingly let the precious moments go in vain. Every living thing in the universe has its own beauty and its own problems. The attitude with which we face our life creates the difference.

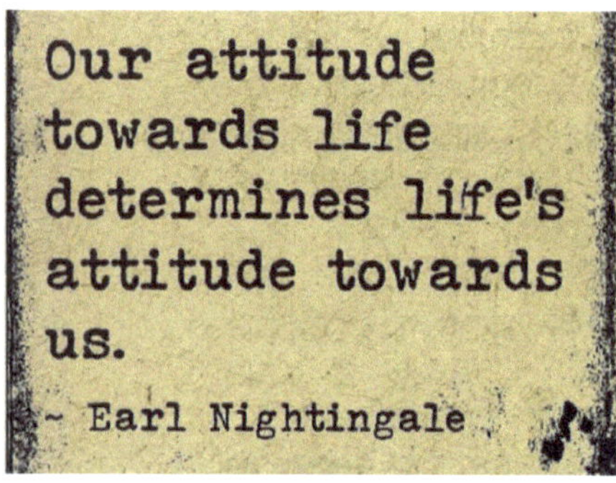


We have to remember that even when we are in pain, we have something inside us which wants to conquer it and live happily and peacefully. Once we realise that our happiness and peace are much larger than our pain, we deny acceptance of the pain. Physical and emotional pains are an undeniable part of the human experience. By denying acceptance, physical pain can be reduced to a level, whereas emotional pain can be eliminated completely.

Our pain can shape us, challenge us, and ultimately guide us toward growth and transformation. The pleasures are as harmful as pain if we try to hold them.

The Bhagwat Gita taught the process of maintaining equilibrium (Stith Pragya) in all situations as the state where neither pleasure nor pain can control us. We dance in pleasure and start weeping in pain. We align ourselves with the incidences. We are not aware of our existence. We should learn to differentiate our existence from the body. We learn to own ownership, which is the best learning out of our existence. This particular learning itself teaches the purpose of existence.

Let's understand the purpose of existence from a religious perspective. The purpose of life suggested by Hindu scriptures is to achieve four aims called Purusharthas. These are dharma (moral life), artha (material prosperity), kama (pleasure), and moksha (liberation) so that we can lead a life of happiness and fulfilment in balance with the universe. It is also interesting that the four paths in life aren't just about spirituality. The second and third goals are really about daily life, specifically, living a purposeful and pleasurable daily life. We are supposed to be happy, wealthy, and successful. Although Moksha is a central concept and considered the ultimate purpose of existence, each goal has its own importance and collectively becomes the building block of a meaningful life.

Many Hindu sculptures suggest the law of karma governs the endless cycle of life, death, and rebirth so that we can attain moksha and free our soul from the struggles and pain of the material world, and liberate the soul from everything. Sometimes, even I felt when the Supreme power is so powerful, why had it not awarded moksha to everyone without even coming to earth. Why negative thoughts generate in our mind which leads to karmic account mismatch?

The best answer I got is in Hindu sculptures, which describe the purpose of the creation by super power is just LEELA. It is a play without any intention. That is the beauty of life. It does not have a specific purpose; flowers don't have a reason to blossom. Machines have purposes, not lives. To make the game fair, the super power may have opted for the law of karma. It has nothing to do with pleasure/ pain, good/bad, and right/wrong. Pleasure for one may be pain for another; good for one may be bad for someone, and right for one may be wrong for others, as they all are subjective perceptions.

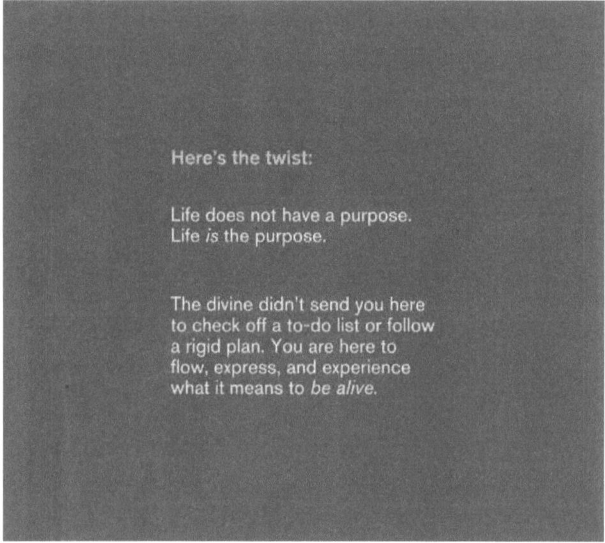


We have not to become something or to achieve something as we already have everything within ourselves. We should always work for excellence, the best version of ourselves, to optimum utilization of the energy that lies within ourselves. The conclusion is only that don't let anyone become master of you, not even your body, mind, senses, habits, and dreams. We should have dreams to touch the moon but at the same time, should not be disheartened if not able to even jump despite our best efforts. Chase your dreams and work hard while preserving with the understanding that dreams are of yours; you are not of dreams. Don't even let your dreams bond you. The less bondage we have, the closer to our real selves we live.

Bondage is the desire/expectation for the future and the regret for the sins of the past. We have tied the bondage, not the bondage has tied us. We have created different filters/bondage at our mind level. In reality, there is no bondage at all. We untied the knot of bondage every night to perceive the contentment lies in the thought-free state of sleep. If the bondage has tied us, we will not be able to untie the knot. Just like we untie the knot to go to sleep, we have to learn how to untie the knot forever. The more we try to see reality through the filters of our desires/expectations, the harder the bondage will be. We should learn to see reality as it is. Reality is not harsh; our expectations make it harsh.

If we want to find our true purpose of existence, we must see our own life from a broader perspective of the whole world and see ourselves in relation to it. Our purpose of existence should not be separated or disconnected from the rest of the world.

We will find the true answer only when we include others in it and align ourselves to the larger aims and interests of the world and all life on earth. The world thus thrives upon the collective action of all. When we all do our parts, we create harmony, spread peace and happiness and make the world a better place to live, we experience a better world inside ourselves as well. It helps in aligning our purpose of existence with the meaningful life. Our main purpose for the existence of human life on earth is to live life with excellence, serving nature or serving the larger aims of creation to give meaning to our as well as other lives and attain cosmic consciousness to become one with the God residing within ourselves.

# 04

# Role of Religion

We, the human beings, are the result of the evolution process of billions of years. The human brain has been developed and eventually we have the capability to think for the last approx. 50,000 years. The philosophy starts from the last 3,000 years when we started getting sufficient food, then the people first got to think about life and the creator. All the philosophies about the creator are very much affected by the experiences of this world, but the reality is that our planet is not more than a decimal point in the cosmos. On the basis of a few thousand years' experiences of life on the decimal-sized planet, we have made religion and large theories to define the creator.

Religions and subsequent theories have been formulated to give purpose to life, reinforce stability, promote psychological well-being, and motivate people to work for positive social change through the incarnation of God in every form of life. But we can never search out the creator merely based on the theories. The only place to meet with Him is our body where he resides. Religion is the way through which we can have interaction with the real self.

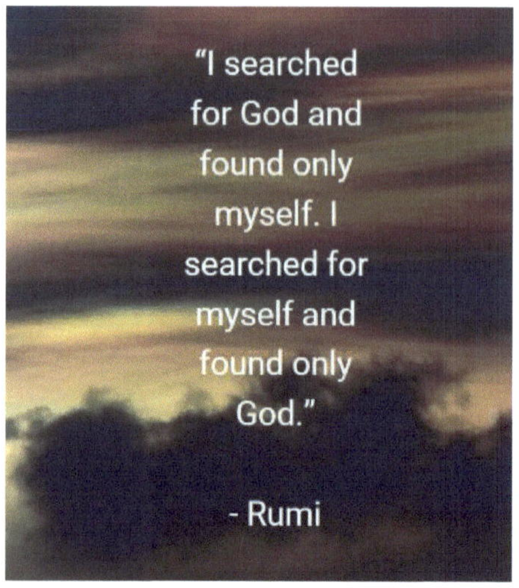


Religions pave the way of life towards the creator, and people often consider the creator as the destination. But if that had been the scenario, the creator need not have sent us on the way; he would have held us right there with him in the so-called heaven. He has sent us into life so that he can experience his creation right from ground zero. Instead of connecting with the infinite and experiencing the infinite, people build walls around the religion and confine everything between heaven and hell.

Moreover, the notion of the creator is contradictory for different religions. The conflict starts when one takes the theories of religion without practically applying them to know the real self. Then, we start believing in God and try to find Him in the outer world with the torch of religion. We forget the torch works only if the light falls on the right object. We are all searching the infinite without turning the torch to the right side. We don't even need a torch or eyes to see Him; we have to only connect with Him as He is within us.

There are several ways to connect with the infinite. We can connect with the almighty through devotion, meditation or detachment. Devotees often have deep and personal experiences of his grace and blessings, ranging from sudden surges of love to powerful senses of his presence everywhere. Devotion seems the easiest way to come closer to the creator. But one cannot become a devotee at one's will. The creator chooses the devotees to bless. Mira Bai, a 16th-century Indian princess and poetess, was a perfect example of a devotee.

Meditation is the moderate way. It starts with self-awareness and ends by knowing the real self. Everything is residing within that finite space. Just remove the colour of selfishness due to which water is boiling. We see the real self which is the same in everyone. Moreover, the creator has opened the doors to know the infinite through self-awareness for everyone without any bias.

Detachment is the art of enjoying something while always being open to the possibility of losing it someday. Detachment by merely avoiding something is just an escape and the easiest way. Real Detachment has nothing to do with other people and things. Detachment does not mean not caring; it is taking care of the real self, which is the same,in everyone. It helps in shifting the self-centric approach to a cosmic-conscious approach. Detachment is not leaving things. It means to see while awakened that nothing is mine.

Just like we have parents to nourish in the apparent world, we all have God as the parents of the subtle world to connect with the real self with Supreme energy/ creator. Religion helps us to connect with our roots. We may connect ourselves with the creator through devotion, self-awareness, or by detaching the false identity of self as all the ways lead to realising that our soul and God's soul are one.

The blessing of devotion is given at the discretion of the creator. Knowledge and self-awareness are dependent on the curiosity in the seeker's mind, and detachment comes automatically if someone either surrenders in devotion or swims through the water with self-awareness. Self-awareness is the best way for all to reach the creator and know the infinite. It is only self-awareness which can transform the belief in the creator into an experience of the same.

The role of religion is to clear the mind to see beyond the mind and experience the infinite universe residing in a finite body. Right knowledge of religion opens the gate for the creator residing within ourselves. Any religion which liberates you is the right religion, but if it confines you, it is neither good nor even a religion at all. The ultimate purpose of religion should not be merely believing in the infinite but to know and experience the infinite residing within us.

# 05

# Power of Mind

The human brain has 100 billion neurons, each neuron connected to 10,000 other neurons. Although the brain controls a person's movements, emotions, and various bodily functions, it is only the mind that alludes to a person's morality, reasoning, and understanding. The mind is much more than the brain. Our super-efficient brain works for the mind. It is because of the mind only that humans are considered as the most intelligent living organisms on earth.

Mind is the best gift of the creator to the humans. The animal has the brain but it is the mind which creates the difference. The mind is a pure vibrating energy and the brain is just a physical manifestation of the mind. The brain is simply the coordination of movements, feelings, and different functions of the body whereas the mind helps us to think, imagine, remember, will, and sense. The mind is also associated with sensory and non-sensory experiences, which include perception, pleasure and pain, belief, desire, intention, and emotion. Broadly, the mind can be categorised into conscious, subconscious and cosmic conscious states. The awareness about these states uncovers the battles your mind goes through and the way out how to align our thoughts and action to conquer the mind.

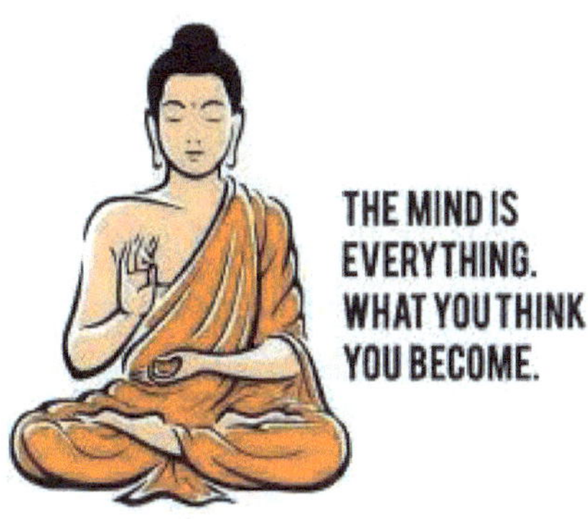


Let's understand the mind with the analogy of the iceberg in the sea. The mind is like an iceberg and is made of 3 parts: the conscious mind (above water), the subconscious mind (just below the waterline), and the cosmic consciousness (way below the waterline). These three parts of the mind define the Level of Awareness of the mind.

The conscious mind is the knowledge which we have acquired from the school, universities, societies, people and our environment. Conscious mind contains all of the thoughts, memories, feelings, and wishes of which we are aware at any given moment. This is the aspect of our mental processing that we can think and talk about rationally. When we dream about the future or get nostalgic thinking of the past, it is the conscious mind that's at work. Conscious mind is consisting of all the mental processes of which we are aware. The conscious mind thinks in terms of the past and future rather than the present. There is no life in the conscious mind. It is just a robotic part of the human body. This is somehow what artificial intelligence is trying to achieve.

When we go deep inside from the conscious mind, we observe the subconscious mind, which is the primary source of human behavior. It contains thoughts and feelings that a person is aware of or not currently aware of, but which can be brought to consciousness. This is a reservoir of feelings, thoughts, urges, and memories that are outside of our conscious awareness. The subconscious mind is like a huge memory bank. Its capacity is virtually unlimited, and it permanently stores everything that ever happens to you. Our feelings, motives, and decisions are actually powerfully influenced by our life experiences and stored in the subconscious. The subconscious mind contains not only past experiences but also your deepest desires/fears that we may not be aware of. Our subconscious mind is constantly focused on the present moment and drives our actions through emotions such as love, fear, and anger.

The subconscious mind is far more powerful than the conscious mind and can process huge quantities of information that come via your five senses and translate them back to your brain in the blink of an eye. The conscious mind is the knowledge, whereas the subconscious mind is the experience of life. The conscious mind is something totally outsider whereas the subconscious mind is the experience of life and also the bridge through which we can get the experience of self.

Undoubtedly, the conscious mind is very essential for the mental development of the human being and for earning money. With the help of knowledge, we can plan better, we can earn money, and with money, we can have a comfortable life.

The conscious mind can give us success but cannot assure excellence, peace, happiness, and contentment in life. We should not give the ownership of self even to success; success should not be larger than us. Success is smaller than life. With the ego of success, we cannot experience our subconscious mind and the real self. We may have developed over the centuries, but inner peace and contentment have decreased due to the negligence of the subconscious mind.

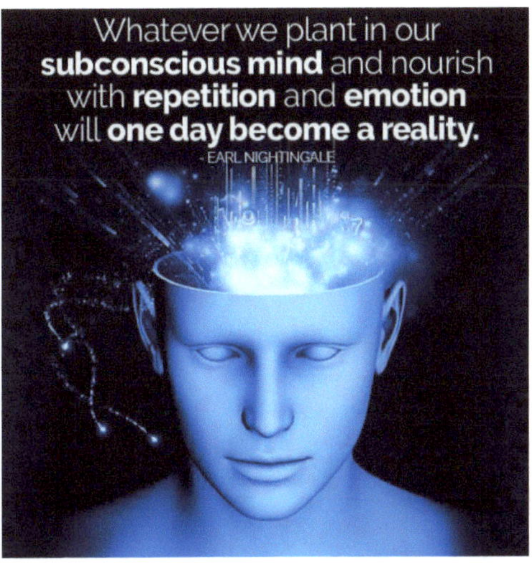


The subconscious mind is the door to cosmic consciousness. When we align our conscious mind with our subconscious mind, the door is opened. The cosmic consciousness is the most important part of the mind and the very basis of our existence.

The cosmic consciousness is a perfect awareness of the oneness of life. We feel that the universe is filled with one life, and the whole universe is ours. It has tremendous treasures, all the memories and experiences of all our past lives. It is collective and cosmic unconsciousness. It has the ability to know something without using the ordinary five senses of sight, hearing, smell, touch, and taste. Cosmic consciousness is extrasensory perception which is basically our sixth sense, a keen intuitive power, a power of perception beyond the five senses.

The Bhagavad Gita describes the cosmic consciousness as "Akshara," meaning the Imperishable One. Just as ocean water can fill into a container of any shape or size, this Supreme Atma too fills itself into the beautiful cups of our imagination purely for our joy and bliss. Each cup is captivating because the consciousness is the same. ***The Universe is the creation of the mind. Universe exists inside the mind as the flower exists inside the seed.***

We all are the bubble of different shapes but all are made of the same water. We are not different. Different people are the mirror of the different thoughts which we have in our minds. We should break the walls of the self and identify ourselves with all the existences of the universe. We are not mind or body, but the informing and sustaining soul, silent, peaceful, eternal, which possesses them; and since we find this soul everywhere sustaining and informing and possessing all lives and minds and bodies, we cease to regard it as a separate and individual being in our own. Having this, we possess our eternal self-existence at rest in its eternal consciousness and bliss.

We can never reach that deep with the help of the conscious mind. The conscious mind has some limitations; it can think and imagine up to the level of the conscious stage. It is only the bridge of the subconscious mind which allows us to get the reflection of the state of cosmic consciousness within ourselves. We have to work on our subconsciousness, mould and align our basic habits and way of life with the creator to achieve cosmic consciousness.

We are just conscious of being in the presence of God and seeing the light of God's countenance. It is the highest state of consciousness with a cosmic or universal understanding. It is the state wherein the experiencer of the different lives differentiates itself from the experiences of different lives. This is the state of "Pure consciousness" wherein the mind has emptied itself of all particulars, objects, images, memories, experiences, and we get aligned with the creator or Supreme energy. This is what meditation is all about.

To attain cosmic consciousness, we have to go through the subconscious mind in an awakened state. In this process, many a time the mind falls into the trap of the conscious mind. We can overcome this with the help of meditation. Meditation is the ship in the ocean to shift the fixed mindset towards growth oriented mindset. It helps us in attaining the self-ownership and once we become master of ourselves, we truly become the architect of our destiny.

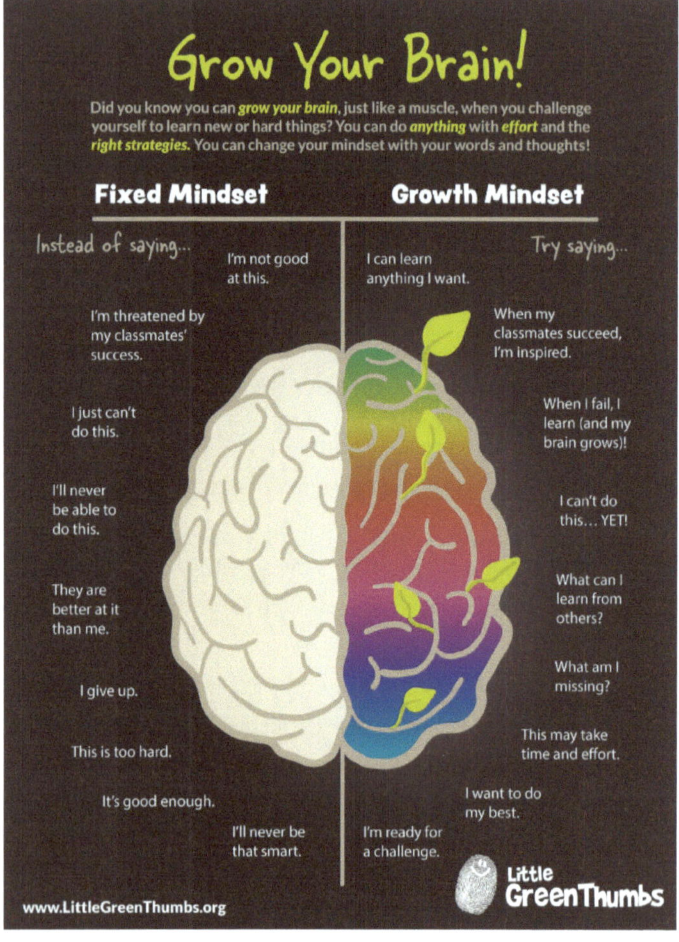

# 06

# Meditation

In its simplest terms, meditation is being fully present with what you are experiencing in the current moment. It can be experienced at any point in time while we sit cross-legged with our open or closed eyes, while staring at a distance while driving, observing natural scenery, listening to someone, talking with someone, dancing, singing, walking or even staring blankly at a wall while waiting in a long queue any time! We are fully engaged in experiencing the moment; all our concentration is on experiencing, and we don't have a single thought, not even regarding the experience we are living. It is simply living in the moment with the inner self.

We all have, knowingly or unknowingly, experienced that moment at some point in time. But such an experience of inner joy usually stays for those particular moments/ minutes/hours. If we try to run after the experience, it will become a trap. Meditation is all about making that experience a permanent part of our lives with the help of self-awareness. Meditation is basically the awareness about the body, mind, thoughts, emotions, senses, and feelings to become the observer of the self and life. If we have a basic awareness of our actions and their consequences, learning from our mistakes, then we are already in a meditative state.

We just have to become the observer of our life, our thinking, and ultimately the observer of ourselves. We just have to ask questions with curiosity. Meditation is all about coming out of emotions, removing the lens of desires and expectations and seeing reality as it is.

We can simply start by observing our life. We have to observe our bodies, our education, our skills, our passion, our capabilities, our society, the surrounding market, the needs of the society and our life. It includes everything from working on the body for flexibility and strengthening the body, working on education to achieve knowledge, working on skills and passion to achieve success, working on enhancing capabilities to attain excellence to ensure physical, mental and financial stability in life. This is also known as karma yoga. The right observation of life will help to achieve success to live healthily and wealthy. It will also test our observation skills. Although success and money never guarantee mental peace, but it is very essential. This is the real foundation of meditation. If we cannot do the basic observation, all other things peace, happiness, and spirituality will become secondary. If the body is sick, then how will we earn money? If one has immense wealth but not health, then it is of no use. Money does not cure any disease. Only if we are healthy and wealthy will we be able to enjoy life.

The next stage of meditation is to know the mind and understand how it works. It includes understanding what the feelings, emotions, and thoughts are and how they affect our life. The practice of self-awareness is suggested to focus our attention and eliminate the stream of jumbled thoughts that may be crowding our minds and causing stress. The concept of self-awareness is based on the idea that we are not our thoughts but the owner who is observing the thoughts; we are the thinker, Separate and apart from our thoughts. We are more than our thoughts. We don't have to control our thoughts; we have to just observe them. Experts estimate that the mind thinks approximately 50,000 thoughts a day. If we pay attention to our thoughts, we will be amazed to discover that most of them are useless, unimportant thoughts that pass through the mind at a huge speed. These are words we repeat in our minds, comments the mind makes, repeating what we heard said, questions, answers, and a lot of senseless wandering thoughts that we might not even be aware of. Subjectively, our thoughts come from nowhere: they just pop into our heads. Objectively, we can say that thoughts are the reflections that emerge out of the permutation and combination of knowledge, belief, ideas, experiences and the outside environment, which includes everything. When our eyes are open, we automatically see the whole frame regardless of good or bad things, but after seeing it, it is our choice whether we have to look at it thoroughly or skip it. And moreover, the nature of the thing will not affect the eyes. Similarly, when our mind is active, thoughts will come automatically, but we have the choice to selectively accept/reject the thoughts. This is the role of the thinker.

Being thinkers, we should never judge and categorise thoughts as good and bad; just become the observer and sit at the bank of your mind and see how the mind is playing. Never suppress any thoughts; rather, use our knowledge and experience to answer the thought.

We have to be just aware of thought. Our thoughts will eventually turn into habits, routines, impulses, and reactions. Our thoughts are random, but our thinking should be selective. The thoughts are streamlined by the thinking, which starts once we give acceptance to the thoughts. We have to streamline our thinking towards constructive means.

Once we streamline our thoughts, our subconscious mind works on autopilot mode. The problem starts when we are aware or forget that we are the pilot of our mind; and then we no longer control our thoughts; rather, they control us.

The more we stay with the question regarding the role of the thinker, the more clear understanding we have. The solution to every problem lies in the problem, but we are always interested in the solution and not the problem. We choose to escape from the problem instead of understanding the problem. This is the real problem.

When we go more deeply, the last stage of meditation comes, which is to know the real self and realise that our soul and cosmic soul are indifferent. Once we know that we are a part of the creator, we automatically move on the path of surrender. In fact, Meditation is an act of surrender and the single most powerful tool on our spiritual journey. Surrendering is a profound act of placing our trust in someone much greater than ourselves, someone who is the source of peace and happiness, our creator. Within the depths of our hearts, we recognise the limitations of our own understanding. We acknowledge that our perspective is often clouded by limited knowledge. Surrendering is not giving up on God or ourselves; it is to trust Him above the situation and become humble. It is an invitation to relinquish control and place our faith in the One who knows the beginning from the end. We find a peace that surpasses understanding, knowing that we are not alone in navigating the intricacies of life.

Surrendering allows us to experience the blessings that await us when we release our grip and let God lead, a surrender of our own limited perspectives. In this act of surrender, we find true freedom and peace. We release the burden of trying to figure everything out on our own and instead embrace the assurance that God is in control. It means entrusting our lives, our plans, and our future into His capable hands. It is when we do not ask anything from God, neither from mouth nor from mind. When we just surrender ourselves and understand that whoever is listening to our prayer knows everything and is not an outsider, rather he is within ourselves.

Prayer is a silent surrendering of everything to creator. There is no need to beg anything in return as when we beg for anything, it makes the prayer heavy and we get separated. We have to just align our soul with God's soul to attain cosmic consciousness and oneness of life. We will feel that the universe is filled with one life and the whole universe is ours. This is the state where we find ourselves aligned with the creator and experience the creator inside ourselves. This is what meditation is all about.

# 07

# Magic of Gratitude

In the hustle and bustle of daily life, sometimes it's too easy to block out the details of the day, forgetting that each and every day holds precious gifts. From the air we breathe, the family we live with and the friendships we hold close, there is always something to be thankful for. Do you remember to thank God for the good things in your life, big and small? The birth on this planet is like winning a lottery in itself. The cosmos has blessed us with the Cosmic Lottery by giving us an opportunity to come onto planet Earth in human form. An uncountable number of tiny details in our cosmic history have made the difference between us being here or not. Things happened just right in our cosmos. If the earth was just a little farther away or a little closer to the sun, then it may never have become suitable for life. There are so many things that could have prevented our lives from ever happening. So many puzzle pieces had to come together in exactly the right order to create our lives. Our existence is immeasurably unlikely.

We can understand it simply by probability theory. There is one chance in 100 trillion that the earth should exist. There is one chance in 1000 billion that life should have evolved on earth. There is one chance in 100 billion that life should have evolved into mankind.

There is one chance in 7 billion that your parents should ever have met and got together. There is one chance in 100 million that you should have been the lucky sperm that met with a fertilised egg. It is incredible and unimaginable, but it is happening anyway. We are alive. The miracle which makes our life possible is a blessing in itself. We don't need a miracle; we are the miracles. We are blessed with a body made of Panchtatva and have the blessing to breathe, feel sensations, think, walk and have a wonderful planet to live in. We are part of and the result of an epic cosmic evolutionary process.

The cosmic evolutionary process that has given birth to us is full of magic and worthy of reverence. The cosmos has blessed us with so many gifts in our life. We should focus on what we have, maximise these gifts and allow them to help us to bloom into our full potential. We should have a list of the blessings of which we are unaware. It should start from scratch. We are blessed with a body made of precious 'Panchtatva'. Additionally, we have adequate food to eat and shelter at home. It is the great favour of the universe. Our cosmos supporting our basic existence is more than sufficient and we should have gratitude to the Supreme energy for everything.

We should be thankful to God every day for waking up in the morning and for the opportunities we have to make a difference in our lives as well as others. We should also be thankful for the struggles that we have overcome because they have made us who we are today. We should also be thankful for the people who love us because they are the ones who make life worth living.

# Gratitude is Magic!

Gratitude lets the Universe know
what you would like to see more
of. Appreciate what you can be
grateful for, and open your heart
to even more goodness in your life!

But the normal human tendency is to focus on what we are lacking. This is not wrong, but people implement it in the wrong way. We should grow ourselves to overcome, and the focus should be on the growth, not on what we are lacking. The whole marketing team of this world focuses on telling what we are lacking, and after that, they offer short-term remedies for the virtual problem. We so often get caught in a "lack trap", focusing on what we don't have. It takes us away from the gratitude. This blinds us from noticing all the abundance in our lives and keeps us away from tapping the abundance.

I want you to reverse the process to see the magic. First of all, be thankful for all the things that you don't want to happen and do not happen. Secondly, be thankful for the problems of life which bring the ocean of opportunity with them. There is no point in having a complaint with the creator as all our problems are man-made. Similarly, all our complaints to people are due to our unrealistic expectations. If we focus on complaining, it will increase dissatisfaction in life, which will lead to a miserable life. I will suggest replacing the complaining with gratitude. I am not saying not to work on the problem, but we should have a solution-oriented approach. Our gratitude builds our faith in ourselves and in the universe as we are part of the universe. Our faith builds our future. Our days are better when we focus on our blessings more than our problems. Be thankful for the smallest blessing you have and you will find that God has already given more than what you deserve. We have to make ourselves more deserving to further unlock the potential of the infinite universe.

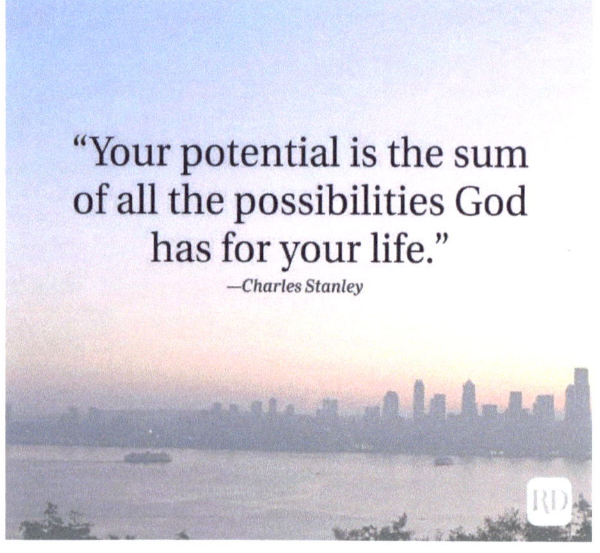

Gratitude is a special gift given to us by God. Gratitude is fundamentally about not taking things for granted. It is being thankful for what we have and receive. Thankfulness is a powerful means of drawing near to God. Be grateful to the universe for providing an opportunity to grow. I remember the famous quote by Ms Helen Keller, "I cried because I had no shoes until I met a man who had no feet." Gratitude can alter negative thoughts, help relieve anxiety and lessen the stress of our daily life. Gratitude has the power to improve our physical, mental, and emotional health. Gratitude, even in a time of difficulty, helps us to stay positive and thankful rather than the opposite of it.

Be grateful for whatever you have and always pursue growth. You are present in this world, which is itself the greatest blessing and use that blessing to make yourself better than yesterday. You have life inside you with infinite power. Every day we must develop the reflex to connect to those gifts, be grateful for them and be proud of where we are at. Research studies have shown that gratitude makes us happier as it has a lasting positive impact, which reduces stress, increases self-esteem, and improves relationships. The ability to be grateful is a great blessing and can actually change one's entire frame of reference and mood. No amount of regret can change the past. No amount of anxiety can change the future. But any amount of gratitude changes the present. "Thank you" is the easiest and best way to express gratitude.

When we express extreme gratitude to the universe with surrender to the universe at the same time, it becomes the best prayer and the most powerful tool against worry, doubt and fear. Always pray to have eyes that see the best, a heart that forgives the worst, a mind that forgets the bad, and a soul that never loses faith.

Prayers are not begging; rather, prayer is the way to connect with God, which already resides inside us. Begging makes your prayers heavy. God knows us much better than ourselves. He knows what we actually need. Let our prayer be so light that the entire universe will become its carrier, and we find every bit of the universe is with us. The highest form of prayer is when we speak neither with mouth nor in mind; we are full of gratitude for everything we have and just surrender ourselves completely to the creator. The moment we surrender to the creator; we stop struggling against existence; existence takes care of everything. The creator approaches us with every single inhale, remains with us while we hold our breath, and we approach the creator when we exhale. Inhale the blessings of the present with gratitude and exhale the regret and anxiety of the past and future through surrender. We can embrace the God within us through a beautiful combination of gratitude and surrender.

Gratitude is a reminder that everything that happens to us comes from God and that we shouldn't take the many bounties in our lives for granted. Gratitude in action is the sense of fulfilment that comes not from wanting more but rather from a sense of knowing that God has already blessed us with what we need. We can put this gratitude into action by helping those who are in need, be it spiritual, emotional, or physical. Gratitude helps us to heal, grow and shine. This is the magical power of gratitude.

# 08

# Law of Attraction

The law of attraction is the most powerful law in the universe. The universal law states that we will attract into our life whatever we focus on. This law determines everything that comes into our lives and everything that we experience. It does so through the magnetic power of our thoughts. With every thought, either consciously or subconsciously, we are creating our future through manifestation. Positive thoughts bring positive results into a person's life, while negative thoughts bring negative outcomes. Whatever we give our energy and attention to is what will come back to us. It works because people and their thoughts are made from "pure energy", and like energy can attract like energy, thereby allowing people to improve their health, wealth, or personal relationships.

When we focus on the abundance of good things in our lives, we will automatically attract more positive things into our lives. But if we centre ourselves on negative thoughts and only focus on what we lack in life, then we will ultimately attract negativity into our lives, and what we want most will continue to elude us. The energy of our thoughts gets manifested at our body level.

Positive thoughts manifest positive experiences and vice versa. This law suggests that similar things are attracted to one another. It means not only people tend to attract people who are similar to them but also people's thoughts tend to attract similar results. As we know, we are the energy hub. We have infinite power in the cosmic consciousness state, the source of energy of our universe. The law of attraction streamlines that infinite energy.

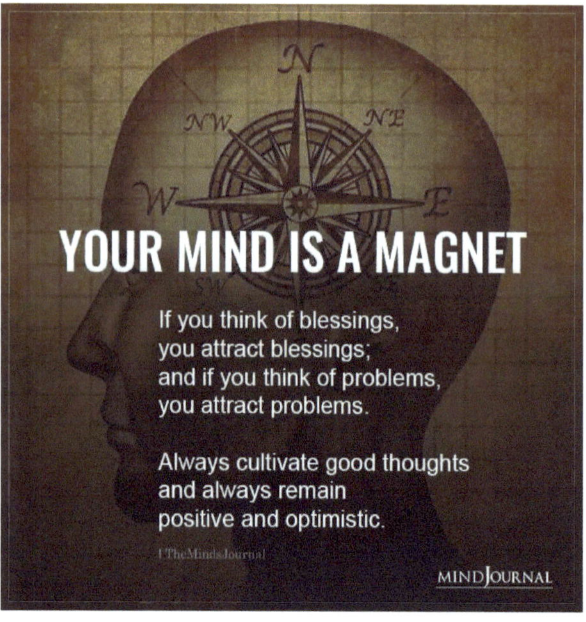


We can avail the power of cosmic consciousness with the help of the subconscious mind. But the subconscious mind has the habit of taking everything literally. It does not differentiate between positive and negative. It always says **"tathastu"**. This means *what you wish for, let it come true*. So, if you continually tell yourself that you will never succeed in a particular venture, it is likely to turn out that way. If you are making positive affirmations out of your laziness, your subconscious mind knows that you are not giving your best, and then it may not work. It works only when you align your mind and thoughts of the conscious mind with the subconscious mind.

The subconscious mind does not think or seek reason independently; it simply obeys the commands it receives from your conscious mind but it ensures that the voice should be right from the inner heart without any manipulation.

We should focus our energy on finding ways to keep our subconscious mind healthy. Our subconscious mind is constantly focused on the present moment. When we dream about the future or get nostalgic thinking of the past, it is the conscious mind that is at work. This is why it is so important to be mindful of inner thoughts in the subconscious mind, such as "I am successful" rather than

"I will be successful". We can manifest positive experiences through the energy of positive thoughts. We are the universe of ourselves, and we have infinite power to bless everyone including ourselves.

But is it practically possible to have positive thinking in every situation? Here, we have to understand the difference between positive thinking and right thinking. Being positive all the time may take you away from reality, and moreover sometimes negative thoughts help us to calculate the risk in advance. In fact, the right thinking is comprehensive thinking, which takes care of both the pros and cons of the matter. But once you decide to go ahead and execute your decision, submit all your negative thoughts to the universe. We should be positive for things that have not happened or things which are not under our control and at the same time, we should have the right thinking for taking actions on the basis of reality.

While the law of attraction may not be an immediate solution for all of life's challenges, it can help us to learn to cultivate a more optimistic outlook on life. It also helps us to stay motivated to continue working toward our goals. It teaches us to focus on what we have rather than what we lack. We have a new day and we are again welcomed by the universe with all blessings. We have to enter a high- energy zone every morning to take action with positive affirmation.

But the positive affirmation doesn't mean to think positively blindly; we have to look at reality first, understand it completely, and do our best to improve ourselves to attain excellence and surrender all worries and things which are beyond our control to the universe to take care of.

We should have positive affirmations for things which are not in our hands. We should ask for favour from the universe for only those things which are beyond our capacity. If we give our best, then the whole universe unites the energy and works for us. This is the law of attracting vibes from the entire universe.

If we learn how to harness the power of the law of attraction, we can direct our thoughts and actions in a way that allows us to effortlessly attract what we want. It starts with seeing the positive in every action, speaking nicely to yourself as well as others and listening to good people and thoughts. Every thought/action is good, which makes us a better person and helps us in improving our capabilities. On the other hand, all the habits which turn us for the worse due to desire or unrealistic expectations are not good habits. Using the law of attraction to improve our capabilities, the universe will give us more than what we deserve, but if we try to use the law of attraction to fulfil only our desires, we will end up 'killing the goose that lays the golden eggs'. Positive Manifestation with the Right Action to make ourselves deserving is the key to matching the frequency of dreams with reality and attaining excellence.

# 09

# Goal of Life

What should be the goal of our life is a single question that has puzzled everyone. The answer may vary from person to person and may be influenced by cultural, societal, and individual values and beliefs. Let's find out the answer which is common for everyone and something which everyone should have. The ways and means may be different, but from the bottom of the inner self, everyone wants to have a happy life. We all strive for happiness. It is the ONLY thing we want for its own sake. Everything else we do is in order to be happy - in one way or another. To live happily, we organise our days, months, years and sometimes the whole of our lives. So, our goals in life should be set in that direction which helps us to attain a happy life. As we get the clue that our goal should be such that it will bring happiness in the long run, let's understand how to find out the real goal of life.

The goal of everyone's is concealed behind the three layers of understanding, and once we penetrate these layers through the light of awareness, we find our real goal. The first layer is to differentiate between need and desire. The things which are actually important for us are essential for us; they are our needs, and the things which we want to influence others are our desires.

Self-Growth is the borderline between the need and the desire. Everything which leads to self-growth is the need of the basic existence, and all others are merely desires. We have to grow not to influence others but for ourselves.

The second layer is to create the inner capacity to receive the blessings of life in order to make ourselves deserving. Life's blessings are abundant, but it's our readiness to accept it, determines if we can embrace them or not. Everyone gets what one deserves, not more than that, not less than that. It may be possible that in a company, the deserving criteria are buttering and you are wondering if your colleague with less qualification gets more promotion than you. Then, you have misunderstood the deserving criteria. In such cases, place yourself in a place where you can justify your qualification. A philanthropist may not be a deserving person for the terrorist organisation, whereas a killer may not be a deserving person for the temple. The criteria of deserving vary from place to place. It's our responsibility to place ourselves at right place.

The third layer is to stick to our basic values. We stick to our basic values to save ourselves from the vicious circle of greed. Greed is just like fire; if we have fire in our hands and hearts, it is we who first get fired, and later, it affects the outer world. The whole world is burning due to that fire of greed. We need to sticks to basics to preserve our vital energy.

*Once we clearly understand our needs, work to make ourselves deserving and at the same time stick to our basic values, it means we have already laid down the roadmap to attain the goal of life. The need varies from person to person, and therefore, everyone has a different definition of a happy life. It's our definition that will determine our destiny.*

In my view, life becomes happier if we are healthy. We should put our mental and physical health at the topmost priority. Mental health includes our emotional, psychological, and social well-being. It affects how we think, feel, and act. Physical health includes the well-being of the body. Good health helps us to think better, to feel good, to feel positive, and to increase productivity. Our good physical and mental health is the key to unlocking the energy from the infinite universe. Then the next target should be to inculpate the power of infinitive universe in our daily life.

We should live life in such a way that it helps us to attain our life's goals, and self-growth is the fuel that makes the flow of happiness sustainable throughout life. Successful people invest their time in their self-growth and personal development. ***Self-growth is a process of both understanding the self and pushing the self to reach the highest potential.*** It involves working on new habits and hobbies, fostering new skills, and practising new strategies. Our goal should make ourselves a better version of ourselves than yesterday. Our focus should be on ourselves, not on others. We need not compare ourselves with other people; rather, we should compare ourselves with who we were yesterday. While this development starts very personally, it radiates outward and touches every aspect of your life, including your practice and professional growth.

The key ingredient of self-growth is to take responsibility and to learn from failures instead of blaming and complaining. We are the creators of our own reality. The universe is conspiring to bring us all that we want. We are here to live a life of fulfilment, and the universe fully supports us in this journey. We need to take responsibility for our lives, keep our vibrations high and watch the magic unfold in our lives. We may experience failures, but we have to remember failure is not the opposite of success but part of success.

Failure builds character. When we face big problems in life, it means the Supreme power is testing highly and gives us an opportunity to do great. Opportunities come with the problem itself. It's our attitude that decides what we choose. When we focus on the problem, it eliminates the opportunity to look outward to find the cause of the problem. *When we stop blaming and take responsibility, we give the message to the universe that I am in charge of our life, and it is the awakening call for the inf inite energy surrounding us.* The entire universe starts working on our behalf.

Our ultimate goal is to make ourselves capable, not merely successful. We often search the growth in success, and most of the time, we are so blind in the race that we don't have any time to think anything else than it. We are so entangled by replacing the basic needs of a happy life with success that no other motive left in our lives. We have to separate it from the desire for success. Success without fulfilment is an absolute failure. We have to focus on improving, not just proving ourselves.

We have to mould our goal of life in such a way that it leads to the attainment of self-growth and excellence in life. It may have reflected outside, but more importantly, we should be self-satisfied and have a sense of fulfilment. *We have to climb up the mountains, not so the world can see us, but to see the world.* We are not here to reach some destination but to have a purposeful journey. Our goal must align with our strengths, passion and the needs of the world so that it gives meaning to our lives. The goal of life is to make our heartbeat match the beat of the universe, to match our nature with mother nature. Great minds think alike because a greater Mind is thinking through us.

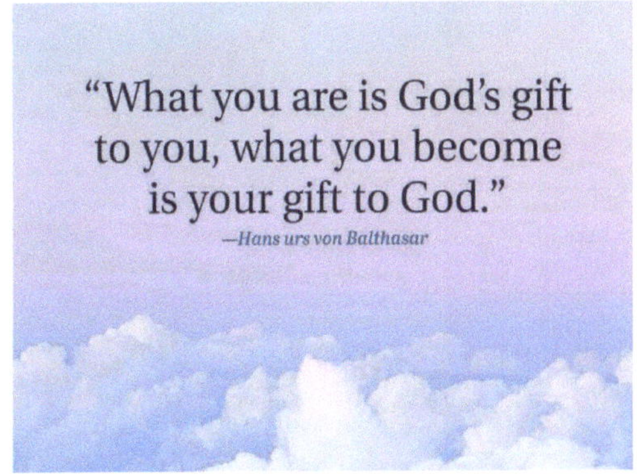

# 10

# Rewrite the Destiny

We are taught to write our destiny with the conscious mind through the knowledge and experiences acquired over the years. It is believed that hard work with discipline opens the door to success and excellence. But when we go deep inside, we find that success and excellence are two different things. Success is about achieving outcomes, whereas excellence is about maximizing the inner potential. We can achieve success through the conscious mind, but the attainment of excellence is possible only with the alignment of the conscious mind with the subconscious mind.

The conscious mind is the architect, whereas the subconscious mind is the vast storehouse for the under- construction project of destiny. Our conscious mind may know that we should quit that unhealthy habit or exercise more often. But this consciousness can only guide in a limited way as it is something outsider. It is the subconscious mind that needs rewiring in order to get the work done through the conscious mind. Because our subconscious mind is our real self and it will sabotage conscious efforts in case of conflict. The more we are aware of our subconscious mind, the better we will become at accessing it. It is only our subconscious mind that helps in manifesting our dreams into reality. Subconscious mind is the beautiful weapon to rewrite the destiny.

Our subconscious mind controls each and every physical movement, whether voluntary or involuntary. Science estimates that 95 percent of our brain's activities, the decisions we make, the actions we take, and our emotions and behaviours depend on brain activity that lies beyond conscious awareness. The subconscious mind does most of the work of our daily activities without us even realising it. Our subconscious mind communicates through images, feelings, and metaphors, focusing on analytical reasoning.

Our subconscious mind is like a kid; it does not know emotions rather than logic or reason. It's the process of the brain that requires no big theoretical speeches, but it is very practical. It doesn't bother about profit or losses and good or bad. We should focus on small habits, how we spend our morning, how we talk to ourselves, what we read and watch, with whom we share energy, and what we eat.

These small habits play a big role in reprogramming the subconscious mind. So we should be very careful for about our small habits.

Let's understand how the subconscious mind works. Whether we are awakening or asleep, our subconscious mind is recording and storing everything. The subconscious is thought of as a biological hard drive. Or like a recorded database for all things about us.

Our subconscious mind never sleeps, rests, or takes a break because it controls all vital processes and functions of the body. Our subconscious mind controls our body, our breathing, our organs' functionality, our cells' growth, and everything. Even when we fall asleep, it is our conscious mind that is sleeping. Our subconscious mind will never fall asleep. In sleep, our conscious mind becomes dormant while the subconscious mind stays fully awake and is solely responsible for the visualisation of thoughts through dreams. We can also understand our subconscious mind better through our dreams.

Our subconscious mind experiences life perfectly when we are in a thought-free state. When we become just the experiencer who is experiencing life. If we suppress our subconscious mind, we are closing the door for cosmic consciousness, the creator, and the creativity inside us. Sometimes, when we relax and put things off for a while, we get a 'lightbulb' moment out of nowhere. It is, in fact, our subconscious saving the day. Our greatest moments of inspiration often 'pop' up from our subconscious. We experience these creative breakthroughs when we are relaxed and not trying to access the part of the brain in which they reside.

Our subconscious mind makes everything we say and do fit a pattern consistent with our self-concept, our "master program". This is why repeating positive affirmations are so effective – we can actually reprogram our thought pattern by slipping in positive and success-oriented sound bites.

Whatever we think in our subconscious mind and speak through the word, it produces the energy in the universe and starts manifesting at our body level. We should be careful while thinking and speaking. The subconscious mind has the habit of taking everything literally without categorising it as positive/negative. It doesn't think or reason independently; it simply obeys the commands it receives.

We need to understand the rules of the mind to reprogram our mindset so that our mind works with us, not against us. We don't need to control our emotions; we just need to pay attention to our subconscious mind and feed it with logical reasoning based on the knowledge of the conscious mind. We need not fight with our subconscious mind to suppress any thoughts or emotions. We don't have to judge the thoughts and categorise them into good or bad, positive or negative. We just need not fight or suppress negative thoughts; we have to learn to think right. Neither force nor suppress the darkness to go away. ***Let the light of right thinking remove the darkness.***

We have to work on our subconscious, mould and align our basic habits and way of life with the creator to achieve the cosmic consciousness. When subconsciousness meets the cosmic consciousness, our thoughts are manifested and have the power to influence our world. We can rewrite our destiny and achieve excellence in life through reprogramming the thought patterns of the subconscious mind. It brings us closer to the whole universe, the creator and the real self.

# 11

# How to Stop Over Thinking

Our thoughts are the fruit of the seed which we implant knowingly or unknowingly out of desire or out of fear. They are just reflections that emerge out of the permutation and combination of the knowledge, belief, ideas, experiences and outside environment which we might not even be aware of. Experts estimate that the mind thinks more than 50,000 thoughts a day. It includes everything from positive to negative, best to worst, real to imaginary, and heaven to hell. The number of thoughts generated is so high and of such a widespread range that many people call it the best gift of the creator, whereas many people want to get rid of the thought itself. The more we think of thoughts, the more we get entangled in them. Instead of judging and categorising the thoughts as good or bad, we should just become observers and sit at the bank of our mind to see how thoughts are playing in the mind. There is a subtle but profound difference between noticing the world around you and letting it affect you. For those who feel a lot, it's easy to mix the two up and get entangle in trap pf overthinking as mixing of both is the foundation of overthinking.

We need to either cut out the observation or let the observation not absorb us. If we opt to skip the observing, it is like limiting the infiniteness and not at all logical. We have to be just aware of ourselves so that we just observe but don't absorb. We should never suppress any thoughts rather use our knowledge and experience to accept or reject the thought. ***If we are not aware of our own thoughts, they will eventually turn into habits, routines, impulses and reactions and eventually turn into undirected missiles.***

When we open our eyes, we see the whole frame and cannot force our eyes to see only the good things. But we can choose whether to look at it thoroughly to process or skip it. Similarly, thoughts may not be in our control but the processing of the thoughts is in our control. So, instead of entangling with the thoughts, we should work on our thinking which is responsible for the processing of thoughts. It is not the thought but the processing that creates the difference. So, it is important to always fast- check the thoughts before accepting them.

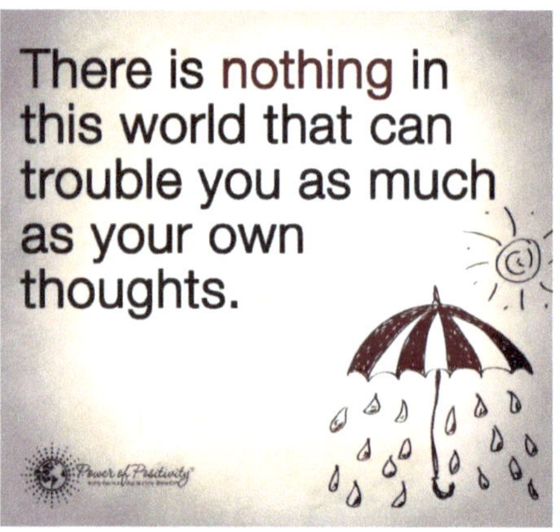


Once we accept the thoughts, they will become ours, and our mind starts processing the chain of thoughts to build our thinking. Our thinking creates our emotions and feelings which will be manifested in our behaviour, which becomes the sources to perceive the external world. Thoughts are like running vehicles on the road of the mind. Vehicles can never be a problem for the road; rather, the road is meant for the passage of vehicles. The right planning is the solution to manage the traffic. Similarly, overthinking is not a problem. Rather, thinking is essential for making a strategy for work life. Right thinking is the key to solving all the problems of our life.

Right thinking requires critical thinking with a positive approach, considering positive and negative thoughts while making decisions. Positive thoughts will push us into a high-energy zone whereas negative thoughts help us to think about the possible risks and help in taking calculated risks and making the right decisions. We have to understand that negative thought is not a problem; rather, wrong thinking is the problem. Blind positive thinking based on unrealistic assumptions and a negative approach to reality are both wrong thinking.

Wrong thinking often results in overthinking, as when the thoughts are based on belief, the chain of thoughts grows exponentially. It starts with doubts and unrealistic assumptions. Negative thinking will create negative emotions and a stuck thought process. It happens if the challenge or issue goes unresolved for a length of time or is so encompassing that it overshadows every other aspect of our lives. It puts us in the trap of overthinking. In overthinking, we create fake scenarios that don't exist. 90% of the harm is caused in our heads by our wrong thinking, while 10% may be the role of reality. Our thoughts will create imaginary scenarios in our minds that reflect our insecurities, fears, and worries. Most of the time, the problem is not the problem. The way we think about the problem is the problem.

It becomes the biggest challenge when we are stuck in the midst of a problem and get caught in a pattern of repeating thoughts and can't let the issue go. This negative thinking chain leads to anticipatory anxiety and creates a vicious circle. To break this cycle, we must learn to break the pattern and stop the anticipatory negative thoughts, then replace the thoughts with more rational, positive thoughts.

Forming new positive habits is hard, but repeating old destructive patterns is also hard. We have to choose our hard. If a person is important, leave the matter, and if the matter is important, let the person go to hell. But never make our mind a dustbin and hold all the garbage there. Our choice of hardness defines and shapes our thought process.

We have to understand that any thinking which is not based on reality is wrong thinking. It can be positive thinking or negative thinking as well. The more we live in the present moment, become unbiased and see the reality as it is, the closer we are to right thinking. Beliefs seem good in the short term because they provide a comfort zone for us, but entangle us in the long run, whereas reality may be difficult in the short run but makes us free in the long run. The chain breaks only when we see the reality beyond our beliefs.

Everything is not black and white in real life. There are many things which may not be clear; in those cases, we have to clear our mindset. In such cases, we should accept the basic fact that perfection is an illusion; no one is only good, and no one is only bad. The worst have some good qualities, and the best may also have some bad attributes. It helps to overcome negative thinking due to over-expectations. It represents an attempt to create new thought chains based on reality. We have to consider the positive and negative aspects of the person, event, or situation in relation to the particular expectation. By accepting reality, we are moving towards right thinking, focusing on our actions and being less affected by the reactions of others.

Right thinking is clear thinking, whereas wrong thinking is blurred thinking based on belief. When we think based on reality, our mind becomes clear, while when we think based on belief, conflicts happen in the mind. The mind with conflict is the problematic mind, and when we remove the conflicts, our mind becomes clearer and lighter, and then we automatically come out of the imaginary chains of thoughts. Once we realise that our beliefs are illusions, negative thinking goes in vain.

Blaming anyone, including ourselves, is the oxygen to the fire of negative thoughts. When we criticise ourselves for past mistakes or see disaster around every corner, just ask one question: "Is there anything I can do to influence the future positively?" If the answer is yes, take an action and rewrite the destiny. If the answer is no, be at peace and submit to the universe.

Accept whatever comes in. No amount of anxiety will change our future; no amount of regret will change our past. Accept the imperfection, accept uncertainty, and accept the uncontrollable. But don't let the level be downgraded. Once we understand it thoroughly, our heads will accept and streamline or reject the thoughts without entangling them. Do the best to have the best and always accept the result. Acceptance of reality is the end of overthinking.

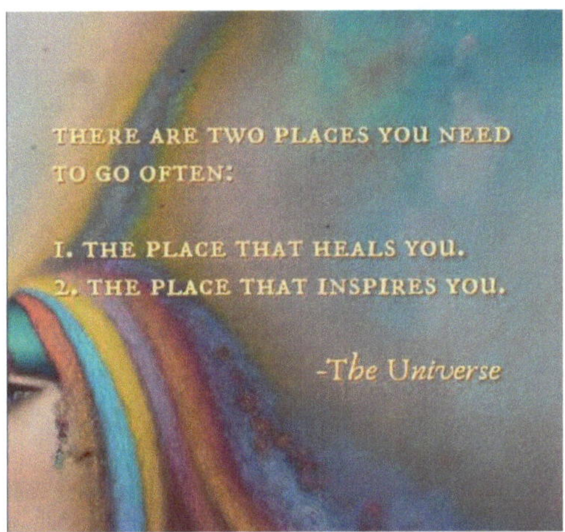

Always remember, the One who creates us will also have the solution for all our problems. Some problems come for improving ourselves, some problems come with a solution, and some problems are meant not to be solved. We have to accept all and understand that different problems are meant for different purposes. We have to understand that overthinking is not a solution, but the right thinking is the solution. We have to apply scientific thinking in life, which means to see reality as it is with the right thinking, the right choice, right action with gratitude for all favours, and surrender to creator for the outcome.

12

# Emotional Intelligence

Intelligence is our basic instinct. Our existence is itself the result of the intelligence of the cosmos. We all are fascinated by intelligence. Everyone wants to become intelligent and run after the cognitive knowledge to become more intelligent. Although cognitive learning helps in learning academic knowledge, it can never assure intelligence and smartness in life. Being intelligent is not about knowing more. If that had been the case, the intelligence of a machine would not be called artificial. What stops that intelligence from becoming real intelligence is the absence of emotions. Real intelligence must be independent; it should be based on logic and should have the freedom of questioning. Intelligence wants to know the reality instead of believing. Intelligence is finding the way in darkness with a torch of knowledge, finding what is right, not what seems right, thinking rightly, not merely positively. When we start questioning, it is the beginning of intelligence.

Intelligence is simply to understand the emotions behind our actions/behaviour, the desires and fears behind those emotions, and apply the knowledge of life to think right, question the thinking to understand the inner self thoroughly, imagine beyond the mind and take rational actions accordingly.

An emotion thinks about the present situation only, whereas the mind thinks about the past and future only. Both emotion and mind are essential. We are being emotional by heart and practical by mind. Emotional Intelligence is to have both but in a balanced way.

Let's find out what emotions are, how they work, how emotions control the mind, how to overcome emotions to unfreeze the mind, how we can use intelligence to build growth-oriented desires to mould our emotions and how emotional maturity helps to convert dreams into reality. In general, emotions are simply the actions or reactions to an event. They are the basic driving force of our actions. They are the architect of the mind and have a substantial influence on our perception, learning, memory, and reasoning.

The mind refines the thought process based on available knowledge. ***Emotions are the navigation, the mind is the engine, and the body is the vehicle in the journey of life.*** Emotions keep us energised for action and moderately activated for life and find out the best possible ways to use that energy. The alignment of all components of the vehicle to push forward in the right direction is intelligence.

***Emotions are guided by desires and fears. We have the power to choose our desires, not emotions. We can have good emotional health by choosing the right desire.*** Once we implant the seed of desire, then the desire works on its own. We cannot choose the outcome. The right desire makes us prosperous, whereas the wrong desire makes our lives hell. The right understanding comes through emotional intelligence, which ensures growth-oriented desire and positive outcomes.

We should start working on our emotions when we are at ease because, at that time, our mind works perfectly. It will bring clarity to our thoughts. It helps us to become self-aware so that we can recognise and understand our emotions, triggers, and patterns of thinking. Self-awareness starts with questioning the inner self, questioning our likes or dislikes, questioning the way we accept or reject, and questioning the way we act or react. Basic questioning helps us reach our deep-rooted desires/fears. Our deep-rooted desires/fears are the foundation of our emotions. We should never suppress our emotions. If we suppress our emotions, we may never come to know our real self. We have to be aware of our desires/fears to mould/replace the seed of desire for healthy emotions in the long run.

Emotional intelligence works until our emotions do not get entangled in an extreme emotional state. Let's understand how the state shifted to the extreme and how to overcome it. Sometimes, something happens, and some of our emotions are triggered, which shifts us to an extreme emotional state (extreme happiness or sadness). Emotions start moving uncontrollably, and the storm distorts the mind. If we observe the situation with intelligence, we find that the trigger is due to a deep-rooted desire or fear inside us. The outside events are just the wind which convert the wind into a storm. We should have self-awareness to come out of the web of emotions, and that awareness cannot be developed in the midst of a storm. Self-awareness is the careful observation of the real self. When we go deep, we find most of the desires are not ours; rather, they are implanted by parents, society, friends, circle, peer pressure, and the market.

Our desires grow automatically based on our outer circle, which includes our upbringing, family background, relatives, friends, circle, and society. Our inner habits, like what we watch, what we read, and what we follow, play a role as a fertiliser in nurturing the seed of desire. Apart from that, the way we think, the books we read, the information we intake, the way we look at life, the way we behave, and live our life are our choices. And it is only our choices which make us or destroy us in long run.

***We are the reflection of our choices. Our small choices of habits make a big difference in life.*** We should have the understanding to prioritise our choices as we have different priorities at different stages of life; it may vary from security, relationship, and success. We can ensure the right fertiliser for the seed by adopting healthy choices. Now, find the right seed of desire with self-awareness. We should take action based on our priority, but the centre point of desire should always be self-growth.

Growth-oriented desire is the right seed of desire. It makes us capable of attaining the highest potential of self. It focuses on becoming the best version of self. It pushes our understanding and limits and breaks the psychological barrier in our minds. These small habits empower us to face negative emotions with all our energy without running away from the pain, suppressing it, or escaping from it. We just face the challenge and allow ourselves to check the upper limit to bear and see our limit and see what it worst and then we realize we don't have upper limit.

On the other hand, the desire to get anything is the wrong desire. The desire to get something will make us a beggar of life. Even if the desire is fulfilled, we become greedy, and if it remains incomplete, we become angry and frustrated with ourselves and jealous of others. The desire out of greed can never make us happy. In such situations, our emotions become fragile and vulnerable. Once we become greedy, whenever the opportunity comes, the mind stops working, and emotions will control us. Similarly, when others succeed, the emotion of jealousy will overshadow the mind. In such cases, the event triggers the emotion in an extreme state because of the wrong desire.

In an extreme state, our happiness pushes us into the excitement zone, whereas our sadness pulls us into a state of depression. When we are in an extreme state, our emotions start controlling us and put the rational mind in the back seat. In this state, we don't act but only react, and that too with an inactive mind. It is essential to put the mind in the driving seat. ***Our mind is like a parachute; it works best when it is open.*** An extreme emotional state we are deprived of the knowledge we have.

In an extreme state, we enter a virtual zone where, instead of observing the root cause, reality, and possible way out, we either start cursing ourselves or blaming others. Wrong thinking fixes us in the trap of emotional pain. It is the hardest time because the pain overcomes us, and we have to come out of this without an active mind.

**In such a situation, the first thing is to accept the emotional pain. Once we accept then the process to overcome starts.** As we understand that the extreme state is not our natural state and it is a temporary feeling, our mind gets reactivated. First of all, Heal the 'I' accept the mistake, feel it, learn from it. Regret is good and it helps to build character. Then, let go of the people and things which are beyond our control. The universe doesn't want the forced outcome. It does not want us to waste our energy in worrying. It wants us to focus our energy on believing, creating, trusting, growing, and manifesting.

Let go of what you cannot change. We should accept that it's okay that there are some things just out of our control. When we choose to let go of things, the whole universe starts taking care of it. We need not worry about the events; we are the actor in the film of life, just make sure to play the role perfectly without judging the role. When we trust the universe, the magic starts happening. It is the first step when the entire cosmos starts working for us.

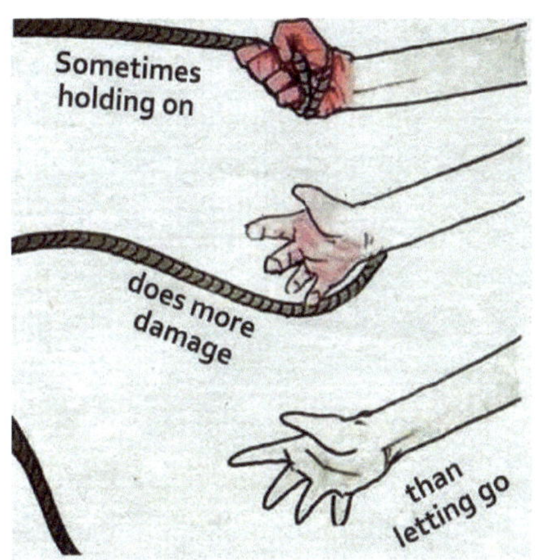

Then, shift the centre point of the emotional pain through detaching with the 'I'. If there is no me, there will be no emotional pain. The more we move away from self-centric thought, the closer we come to the right thinking. Right thinking helps in shifting towards a natural state. *We have to overcome out of the trap without mind. In such a situation, the role of our small habits and clarity of thoughts developed when we are in our natural emotional state makes the big differences.*

Additionally, we should take some prevention so that we do not regret it in the future. We should never make permanent decisions based on temporary feelings; that is why the old proverb says, **"Don't make promises when you are happy and don't make decisions when you are angry."** Instead of working on ourselves, we search out ways to release the pressure built in the mind. Our wrong way of handling the situation makes it worse. Generally, we either choose to share the matter with the convicted person to clear out our stand and get the garbage out generated thereof or with our close group for acceptance, sympathy and guidance.

In the hurry to release pressure, we forget that if we cannot assure someone in our natural state, we can never justify ourselves in an extreme emotional state. Moreover, many a time, we even need not justify our actions. On the other hand, when we share a high emotional state with our near and dear ones, we generally seek acceptance and sympathy. Acceptance makes our state permanent, whereas rejection takes us to a higher extreme end. Then, see the reality that the right guidance comes from expertise, not emotions. The guidance even if we receive it, we are not in a position to execute it due to an absent mind.

Moreover, it is also possible that we are dealing with a virtual problem and such a problem may build pressure on the mind of the person with whom we are sharing. When we shift to a natural state, we easily waive out virtual problems imagined in a highly emotional state, but the person with whom we share may have accepted them as real problems. It may lead to a further chain of problems.

The situation turns worse if the quarrel is a close one itself. In such cases, never ever speak that truth which you have nurtured for a long time and never bring the past into the current fight. In the past, usually, we all have made mistakes, and when we are involved in such a problematic past in a high emotional state, the situation goes out of our control. We forget that we cannot clearly share our standpoint with anyone with an absent mind. So, it is better, from our enemy to friend, not to deal with anyone in an extreme state of mind. It is true that happiness increases with sharing and sadness decreases with sharing, but sharing in extreme happiness and sadness is hazardous for both. To shift ourselves from a high emotional state to our natural state is our sole responsibility. The others can support it, but shifting has to be done by 'I' only.

Once we understand our emotions, we become sensitive towards the emotions of others. It does not mean that we have to fix or save people, to be liked, or to please everyone. **When we see life from a broader perspective, we find that everyone is a happiness seeker.** When we accept the reality, our focus shifts from others to ourselves. We start understanding that if we get hurt, it's our mistake; everyone does everything for the sake of happiness. It means just to come out of the self-centric emotions and have a broader mind which understands the emotions and perspectives of others. This is emotional maturity.

We have to understand whatever happens in life just happens, neither for good nor for bad; it happens just as it is meant to happen. There is no reason. The good and bad are in our minds only. It is just our mindset.

It's our expectations, choices, and perspective of thoughts which think in terms of problem and solution. If there is life, there will be thought, and our thoughts have both the problems and their solutions. Problems in life will never going to vanish. Only the mask of the problem changes, but the problem remains. ***Although life is full of problems, every problem comes with a solution. We have to focus on the solution, not on problems.***

The seed of self-motivation implanted in ourselves at the right time will help us to overcome the problem. We face despair in every phase of life. To keep oneself energised and motivated in that phase is not easy at all. Self-motivation is required in a difficult phase to come out of this and also throughout life to keep pushing us forward. The desire for self-growth keeps us motivated to conquer every problem.

With our emotional maturity, we can not only build our future but can also change the past by re-understanding the event with a broader perspective. ***The small habits of self-awareness, self-love, self-growth, letting go, and submission***

***to the creator will make a big difference.*** The One who creates us will also have the solution for all our problems. These small habits push our limits to realise our inner power.

A big part of our emotional well-being depends on our mindset, the habits we practice, and the way we live each day. The more we are aware of the emotions behind our behavior, the better we can use it to guide our actions in life. We can say that the right approach we adopt to deal with our emotions strongly affects ourselves and helps in creating self-belief, gives positive energy and helps us to pushes out of the extreme situation with ease.

When we choose the right desires, prioritise our choices, understand our emotions with self- awareness, be sensitive to the emotions of others, accept imperfections, think beyond the mind and focus on self- growth, then we use our precious energy to blossom and grow.

# 13

# Theory of Karma

The universe is made of energy, and the energy in everything is in motion. Our Karma, which includes our actions, words, and beliefs, manifests the cosmic energy, and the law of karma governs the energy game of the cosmos. Everything we do creates a corresponding energy that comes back to us. The law of karma describes the concept of getting back whatever we put forth, whether good or bad, into the universe. It's simply the energy game in which the energy we put out is the energy we get back. It is based on the principle of cause and effect, wherein the intent and actions of an individual influence the future of that individual. Every cause has its effect; every effect has its cause.

The law of karma is based on the theory of individual actions and their settlement in life or even through rebirth. But if the law of karma worked exactly, the moral and spiritual existence would have increased and the world would have become a better place to live over the period of time. We should have moved from kalyug to satyug but we have the reverse journey; it means this law has not been interpreted rightly. Moreover, if the creator has such technology to match the accounts of virtue and sin, it should have permanently deleted the sinful thoughts from the software of the mind itself, so that everyone has a sinless life.

Before understanding the in-depth workings of the law, let's understand what karma is all about. Any thought/action which is carried by intention, desire, or motive is karma, whereas any thought/action which is performed without intention is not our karma. ***Karma is all about the intention, not the outcome.*** We mistakenly believe outcome is the deciding factor of the law.

The law of karma actually works on the principle of right and wrong in the mind. Understanding the concept of karma helps us to be more mindful of our thoughts, emotions, actions, and deeds and to live the most aligned life and become the best version of the person we were meant to be. These laws can help you understand how karma really works and the effect that our thoughts and actions can have on us and the world around us.

We think about big theories for the law of karma, but the creator implemented it with very basic functioning. It starts with our thoughts/action or some basic choices. The creator, who has more than a hundred billion galaxies in the universe, may not have the time to judge each and every thought/action of everyone minutely. He has developed an independent system to operate the law. When we do anything, we make small choices; our choices define our habits and our lives as a whole. These choices are the judges in the law. The creator need not come to give an award or punish; the choices will do the work. If some have chosen excellence, failure may come in life, but they cannot take the desire of self-growth, if some choose happiness, sorrow may come in his life but he overcomes it.

If some choose to deceive some, he may get success in the short run but in the long run, he is going to fall into the trap of it as the desire for greed never ends. It is not someone from outside coming and doing the justice; ***Our choices do the justice through law of karma.***

When I saw some kid having mountains of problems in their head, I felt what wrong they had done as they were getting so much suffering. Blaming past life actions does not seem logical. There must be some outside factors which are also responsible. We are not alone here. Everything in creation directly or indirectly affects not only oneself but also others, just as others' actions affect themselves and us. Every person, directly or indirectly, impacts everybody. So, we have to develop the understanding that it is not always our karma which affects us.

Sometimes, we may face challenges or get the fruits without sowing the seed. It may be possible that something wrong happens to someone and the victims as well as the accused have no role in it. This is not karma, it is simply a situation thrown by life but the way we react to it, it will become our karma.

Let's understand, with the help of an example, if someone is hit by a vehicle in a road accident and goes into a coma. Both the victim and the accused may be right in their place, and still the tragedy happens as visibility reduces due to a landslide. In this case, whom do we blame? The victim for their past life karma, the accused, the rain, or the landslide. It may happen without the mistake of anyone. This is just a situation that is presented by life.

Many a time, life presents a situation as a consequence of the actions of others. Till then, we have not done any action, not even created the thought in mind. But the way we react to the situation and label it right or wrong, good or bad, easy or difficult, will become our karma. In reality, it is just a situation. Instead of labelling it, channel the energy to grow out of it. This is the real character of the karma.

The majority of people believe that if something good or bad happens to them, it happens because of their actions of past life. The worst use of the law of karma is cursing anyone. ***The law of karma is meant for taking responsibility and an action-oriented approach to writing the destiny.***

"He who blames **others**
has a long way to go on his journey.
He who blames **himself** is halfway there.
He who blames **no one**
has **arrived**."

Chinese Proverb

The worst interpretation is to look backwards and blame the self or others for the present. Blaming eliminates the opportunity to look forward to finding the cause of the problems. There is a proverb, "he who blames others has a long way to go on his journey. He who blames himself is halfway there. He who blames no one has arrived." When we stop blaming, we take the responsibility and give the space to actions. We have to act to make things happen, as nothing happens magically.

**We are the product of our choices**. Many times, we find ourselves reacting to the world around us, trapped in a back-and-forth of reacting to our circumstances rather than forging our own path. When we take action to get the effect we want, we move from feeling like a victim to feeling empowered. We can change the path of our lives by the philosophy of how to live our lives so we can truly become the best version of ourselves and live the most fulfilling life we can. **In the end, our choices define our character and build our destiny through our karma.**

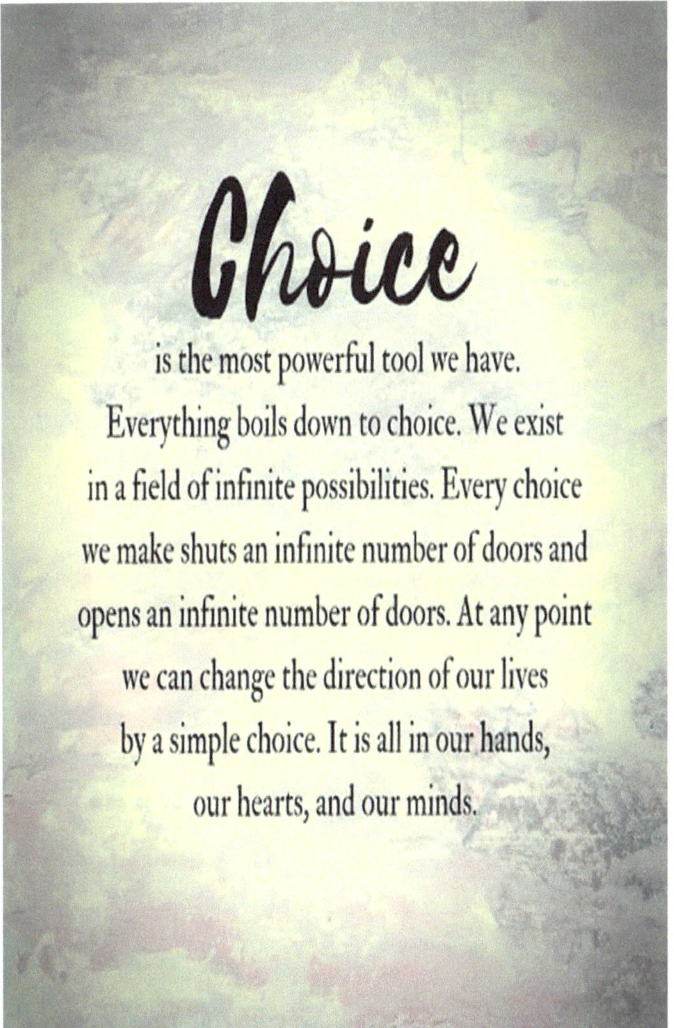

# 14

# Peace and Happiness

Peace and happiness are complementary to each other and related to positive psychology. ***Peace is happiness at rest whereas happiness is simply Peace in Motion.*** Peace is experienced when one is able to put a full stop to the regret/revenge of the past and worries for the future. It refers to the absence of conflicts within, with others, and with time. The inner conflict ends with the alignment of the conscious and subconscious mind. The conflict with others ends when we take responsibility and stop complaining. The conflict with time ceases through gratitude. The universe blessed everyone; the timing may not be perfect for everyone/every time, but if we have the attitude to turn every stone thrown into a milestone, no one can stop us when things become favourable.

Peace is our natural state. This state is always present in everyone. However, when peace is shrouded by conflict, it is not accessible. The absence of conflict is the essence of peace. When we experience conflicts, we tend to complain more and more and eventually end up shrouding peace even further. That is why, at least when we are unhappy, we should put peace first. When we are convinced that peace is the biggest wealth, we won't allow it to get stolen. It is our responsibility to keep ourselves in our natural state during the journey of life. We are not supposed to be peaceful; we are already at peace.

By reminding ourselves and by accessing the peaceful state, we remain the master and do not let the circumstances owe our ownership.

Although external circumstances have an impact on our state of mind, the primary determinant is the way we respond. The more aware we are about the self, the less we are affected by external circumstances. This is nothing but spirituality. ***Peace and happiness are the byproducts of spirituality.*** Actively engagement in spiritual practices lead to a greater sense of self awareness and contentment in life.

When we become aware of the self, we realise that we are the ocean of peace and happiness. We are the owners of that treasure. Experiencing positive emotions is the only way to open the treasury of inner peace and happiness. On the other hand, if we try to seek it from others, merely seeking turns ourselves from owner into beggar. Just as each one understands the importance of protecting and securing wealth, we have to understand to safeguard peace and happiness and to do that, we have to keep an eye on it. Since we are guarding our consciousness, it won't be stolen.

Now, understand the inner layers of happiness. As happiness starts with a peaceful mind, let's understand how we will put peace first. Whenever an incident happens, Ask, 'Do I see this incident as an opportunity or an obstacle'? If, after the incident, the level of consciousness dropped, that means it was a trap. But if we reciprocated in the way a person of a higher level of consciousness, then we should go ahead and pick that opportunity. This will shift us towards absolute happiness in the long run.

On the other hand, when we try to seek happiness in others, we try to be happy through the thought. This is relative happiness, and it is temporary, as thoughts have their own limitations. Our thoughts find happiness through acceptance and pleasure. When we thought to be happy through acceptance of others, we indirectly hand over the ownership of the treasury to others. Moreover, acceptance and rejection are the two sides of the same coin. Similarly, when we try to be happy through pleasure, it means we are depending on sense organs for happiness. Moreover, pleasure has pain along with it, as pleasure and pain are the two sides of the same coin.

When our happiness depends on desires, pleasure and people, it is happiness in relation to a specific outcome based on something external. This kind of happiness can be intense but is short-lived. Moreover, the desire for acceptance and pleasure is always increasing, as we need higher acceptance and pleasure after some time. We get bored with what we have. We always seek more, and if we are seeking continuously, it will put us in a beggar position.

Many people have tried to find happiness through money as it helps in fulfilling desires and pleasures, but we have to understand that although money is very important, it has nothing to do with happiness. Therefore, Money should not be the central point of decision-making for sake of happiness. Like petrol is a must for a vehicle, we need money for survival, but if someone keeps adding petrol reserve and uses all the energy of the vehicle to accumulate the petrol, then we will move away from happiness. The role of a vehicle is to travel. Money gives fuel to the vehicle but never lets the vehicle become a slave of fuel itself.

I have seen people who already have 10 crores and are targeting to have 100 crores at any cost. The target is fine, but if someone keeps the figure in the centre of all decisions of life, then, in my view, that person is nothing more than the beggar of 90 crores. Money can help in attaining relative happiness, that too up to a level for the time being only, but it can never buy absolute happiness.

We should try to go beyond our thoughts and work for absolute happiness. The real happiness is the stage when we are just living the moment. It is removing the curtains of thoughts or seeing beyond the mind. We have been taught that success, name, fame, and money give happiness. Everyone runs after relative happiness, as people have thoughts only up to that level. Whereas in reality, happiness has nothing to do with all these.

I am not saying to leave money and position but just to understand that these are not interconnected. Happiness is pondering inside the real self to taste the sweetness in our own heart. Only after that we may find the sweetness in every heart.

Self-understanding is the key to happiness. Experiencing positive emotions leads to one's inner peace and happiness. The world around us is beautiful when our inner universe is peaceful. We can never see the creator residing within through the boiling water of worries. Water needs to be cooled off to see the creator residing inside the temple of the mind. A peaceful mind sets the eyes on gratitude and attracts absolute happiness.

Absolute happiness does not change with time and people. It involves working for perfection while enjoying the imperfection. Psychologists have labelled this as the ultimate happiness and a call for connection to the larger universe or a sort of transcendence. Some attain this through spirituality or religion, others through philosophy, art or scientific endeavours. The journey may be different, but the destination is the same for everyone, and happiness lies in the experience of that journey. Everyone is set to rest in peace at the destination, but the experience of peace in motion throughout the journey is the real happiness of life.

# 15

# Love and Freedom

The word "love" has distinct meanings in different contexts, but the foundation of love is the same in every context. **It starts with affection, nurtures with attachment and becomes immortal with freedom.** Love is to make a difference in someone's life for their sake, not yours. It takes us toward freedom and liberation. Freedom makes it unconditional and makes it sources of love for the entire universe.

The Creator himself is the purest form of love, and he deliberately radiates it to the entire universe so that all of its creations would become the source of love. The creator reaches every particle of the universe through love. The creator has made us to love and to be loved. He makes a beautiful arrangement through which every living organism is born with overflowed mother's love. **He has blessed everyone with an awesome body which is a miniature of the universe, a beautiful heart full of compassion, and a super mind which can even create the creator.** Everyone is a beautiful expression of the universe and the owner of the treasury of love; each of us is capable of tapping into that treasure.

Then the question arises: if the creator has filled us with so much love, do we even really need others? Let's understand the enigma. We start our journey with self-love. Self-love is the foundation of all love, and as we love and accept ourselves unconditionally, we become a magnet of love and positivity.

We are magnificent beings, and our self-love is the key to unlocking the abundance of love inside us. We are worthy of all the love, so embrace the worthiness of self and let self-love flow freely. Self-love means prioritizing the self, forgiving the self, and being aware and content with who I am.

Self-love starts with self-discipline, not with freedom as the majority of people think. If we are using this body to attain pleasure, then we are not loving the self; we are merely loving the pleasures. When we really love the inner self, we love the creator residing inside the body and, subsequently, the whole of its creation. When we get aligned with our true essence, we become the source of love for the universe. When we celebrate the existence of self, the abundance flows and reflects into our experience, and we attain immortal freedom.

There is an old proverb: "Beauty lies in the eyes of the beholder." It is rightly said that one who cannot love oneself can never love others. The rule is simple: we can give others only what we have. We must own it before sharing it with others. The outsiders are just the reflection of our inner self.

Just like the light needs space to reflect, we need others to have a broader reflection of the real self. We don't need others to accumulate the wealth of love as we already have the reservoir in our hearts.

We need kindness and compassion for others just to reflect the treasure inside us. This wealth increases with the deliberate act of serving, but the moment we seek something in return, the wealth vanishes away. Moreover, if we love someone conditionally, it means we are seeking something in return. Merely seeking turns us from owners to beggars. If someone is begging, it means he is accepting in his subconscious mind that he doesn't have enough. The search for others is nothing more than running away from the real self. And the moment we become escapists, we move away from the treasure. We need others to experience the broader reflection of the creator by serving others, not to seek love in return. The irony is that the seeker will remain the beggar, and the giver always owns the treasure.

When we are content with our inner self, love becomes the key to feeling the reflection of the creator in every particle of the universe. If we are able to find the traces of the creator in our inner self, we have an abundance of love for the self and for every creation of the creator. When our vibrations are pure, our subconscious mind works through the law of attraction and attracts similar energy in abundance. The universe makes the arrangement to bless the giver by making it the source of love. We don't need to experience the creator for the sake of the creator; we need it to unlock the treasure of love for ourselves. Love means spreading happiness without any expectations. It is a one-way flow. It neither bothers nor calculates the return. It is an amazing event. It is not normal; it is illuminated. It is the light of heaven that enters on the earth.

Love is a broad emotion which encompasses everything from attachment and commitment to freedom. People misinterpret it with relationship. Love and relationships are two different aspects. *We have so much love and compassion inside ourselves that the entire universe is small for radiating, whereas one person is more than sufficient to be in a relationship.* Love is the beautiful arrangement of the creator in which the one who radiates it, we become the source of it and experience it in abundance everywhere. In contrast, a relationship is a man-made arrangement to ensure that love and compassion return back.

Love happens without a plan through the subconscious mind in a free flow, whereas a relationship is a planned deal through the conscious mind to streamline the flow of love. For love, we don't need anyone; we can love everyone, from the creator itself to all of its creation, but for a relationship, we need someone to respond. A relationship is a two-sided agreement on how the people will be involved in each other's lives.

For a healthy relationship, love and commitment are both essential. The problem starts when people focus on commitment without love; it converts relationships into bondage. When love becomes the weapon to take possession, the compassion will vanish away. Moreover, when we take possession, we convert our beloved one into a slave. And remember, when we make someone slave, we also become the slave of that slave and fall into the trap of bondage.

Love can prosper in a relationship, but the moment we try to hold the person or moment, the attachment becomes bondage. Attachment binds us, whereas love frees us. Attachment thinks of ourselves first and wants possession, whereas love puts the other one first and thinks for the betterment of the other person. The attachment has selfishness and ego in itself, whereas love wants to attach unconditionally without any expectation in return.

Relationship is a beautiful way to experience the creator or the inner self in another person. But the problem starts when someone enters a relationship to seek love. Rather, we should move into a relationship when we have experienced self-love and have overflowed love to share.

We should go into a relationship when the energy and desire to give outpour within ourselves. The love we seek in a relationship is already within us. If someone comes into a relationship to give love, no one can hurt him. But the problem starts when people come into a relationship to seek love. The situation becomes worse when two beggars meet; then, they become a problem for each other as well as for society.

We need two basic things in life, i.e. love and freedom; everything else is after this. But the possessiveness becomes the wall in between. The mindset to hold the moment pushes us to hold the person. People are just using love as a tool to take ownership of another person. Ironically, the one who has not taken ownership of himself seeks more of such ownership outside. The one who has enjoyed the ownership of self, whether in love or in a relationship, must be self-satisfied, and such a person will never have the intention of owning or ruling.

Attachment is common for love and relationship, but in love, we are attached to others with freedom, whereas in a relationship, we are attached to self with possession. But if someone succeeds in a relationship to the extent that he/she finds the reflection of the creator in his beloved without possession, the flower of love blossoms in the relationship, too.

That unconditional relationship is the miniature of love. Such love inspires us, motivates us, enlightens us, brings us together, and makes us immortal. From a broader perspective, we can conclude that love is devotion. If we really love someone, we find everything in that. Love is also a meditation as it is nurtured by living in the moment in the present, and at the same time love is also detachment as it thinks for others before the self. Overall, love is the free flow of energy to experience the creator and its creation.

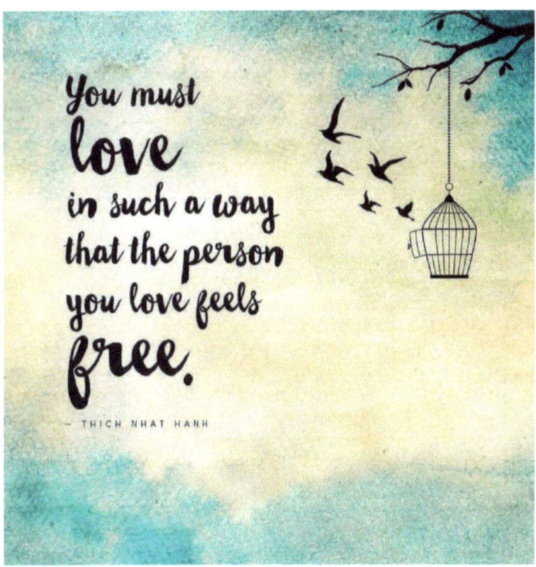

# 16

# Live the Life

Life is the biggest blessing of the creator in the universe. It gives us the dais for the manifestation of infinite and immortal energy. This power makes each of us a unique creature. The creator has placed everyone perfectly in the energy game. It is the limitation of our mind, which thinks of life merely in between the cycle of birth and death. Life is beyond the cycle. Life neither starts with birth nor ceases with death. The opposite of death is not life. It's birth. The form may change and does change, but life never ceases.

If we want to understand life, then we have to understand birth and death. Everything is made of the same source, and everything returns to its original source at the end. Birth is going away from the original source, and death is coming back to that native source. Birth is the forgetfulness, and death is again a remembrance of that source. We have the life to play the beautiful game of manifestation and experience the infinite energy in between. Every experience is a pearl in itself and its positive manifestation helps us to place it righty in thread. The way we manifest things will create us or break us in long run. So we should be attentive as every experience is one-time opportunity. Heraclitus quotes it beautifully, "No man ever steps in the same river twice, for it's not the same river, and he's not the same man."

> LIFE IS AN OPPORTUNITY, BENEFIT FROM IT.
> LIFE IS BEAUTY, ADMIRE IT.
> LIFE IS A DREAM, REALIZE IT.
> LIFE IS A CHALLENGE, MEET IT.
> LIFE IS A DUTY, COMPLETE IT.
> LIFE IS A GAME, PLAY IT.
> LIFE IS A PROMISE, FULFILL IT.
> LIFE IS SORROW, OVERCOME IT.
> LIFE IS A SONG, SING IT.
> LIFE IS A STRUGGLE, ACCEPT IT.
> LIFE IS A TRAGEDY, CONFRONT IT.
> LIFE IS AN ADVENTURE, DARE IT.
> LIFE IS LUCK, MAKE IT.
> LIFE IS TOO PRECIOUS, DO NOT DESTROY IT.
> LIFE IS LIFE, FIGHT FOR IT.
> — MOTHER TERESA

The law of energy also states that energy can neither be created nor destroyed. Then, how do we, the energy of consciousness, could exist or cease to exist? Being the owner of infinite and immortal energy, it's our responsibility to streamline that energy to play the role assigned by the creator to the fullest. We have to implant the right seeds and provide a favourable environment to revive the infiniteness. Growth-oriented desire is the right seed, and keeping the energy positive is the favourable environment for the seed. When we implant the right seed with the power of positivity to enjoy every moment at its fullest, we start aligning with the creator residing inside us. It is not the years in life but the life in years that actually matters.

Do your best with things that are within your control, and don't worry about the things that are beyond your control. Make mistakes, but don't regret them; learn from them. Regrets are the hardest thing to carry and the biggest barrier to growth. The mind never grows in limitation. It grows while we do different experiments and overcome difficulties. Our passion is the best weapon in this mind game.

Passion is the energy flow which helps to overcome challenges with ease. Our passion keeps us positive and motivated for life. **It is a driving force that propels us towards personal growth and helps us to live life to the fullest**. When we are passionate about something, we are willing to invest our time, energy, and resources, enabling us to become the best version of ourselves. We have to identify our passion very carefully. When we implant the right seed and fertilise it with passion, it converts us into a masterpiece. It is the foundation for excellence in life.

We need excellence for ourselves. We should have dreams of touching the moon but, at the same time, should not be disheartened if we are not able to even jump despite our best efforts. Life itself is not more than a game to play. Always remember that playing is more important than winning in the game of life. The moment you play the game wholeheartedly, you have already won the game, whatever the result may be in the game of life. The result is important for others, but the trying is important for the inner self.

We can't change everything that happens, but we can choose how to react to it – and in the process, shape our destiny and create the most incredible life experience. Follow the golden rule "Jab koi baat chhoti kre, to apna dil bda kro".

It makes life easy. Accept the situation, change the situation or leave the situation, but don't let the healer be in pain. There are different ways to heal the inner self, such as spreading happiness, meditation, or simply being in a grateful zone. In all three situations, we are connected with the real self. Spreading love and happiness is the easiest way to recharge the energy. Whenever in a position to help someone, be glad and always do it because that's the universe answering someone's prayer through you. And once we become the carrier of the prayer, we move towards the infiniteness, toward our best version, towards heaven.

Heaven is in life, not after life. Heaven is where life is dancing in thousands of colours and singing thousands of tunes. If we miss it while living, how do we get it in the afterlife? **Heaven comes out of life, not out of death.** We should embrace the festival of life and celebrate it to the fullest. We are so lucky that we don't even realize it. The breath that we just took is a blessing. Embrace each and every breath whole heartedly. We have no idea that there are millions of people in the world who are dreaming of living a life that we are living right now.

We should follow two simple principles to live life to the fullest. First, live every moment of life as if it will not come again, and second, live life with the understanding that the game of energy is never going to cease. *We are here to live the temporary moments with permanent energy.* We should make the most of every moment without degrading the energy of the soul. Life is all about finding the equilibrium between both ends.

We have to work with our inner self to attain equilibrium. Life can only be understood backwards, but it must be lived forwards. We have one life, and it is our duty to make it large. Life is not short; rather, we start living very late. In some cases, it never starts. Don't live the same year 75 times and call it a life.

The only sin in life is not to live life. We have good and bad days, and the most important thing is to live life king-size, regardless of how good or awful days are. We all have the power to convert our dreams into reality. When we live the life king-size, we are not only giving meaning to our life but also facing the fears with courage and an open mind.

It will take out the fear of death inside us. Death is beautiful only for those who have lived their life beautifully, who have not been afraid to live, who have been courageous to live, who loved, who danced, and who celebrated; death becomes the ultimate celebration. Whatever our life is, death reveals only that. If someone has been miserable in life, death reveals misery. Death is a great revealer. If someone has been happy in his life, death reveals happiness. We really don't need more time before death; what we need is more life during the time we are given. Life is not a problem to be solved but a reality to be experienced. Celebrate it and create the life of dreams.

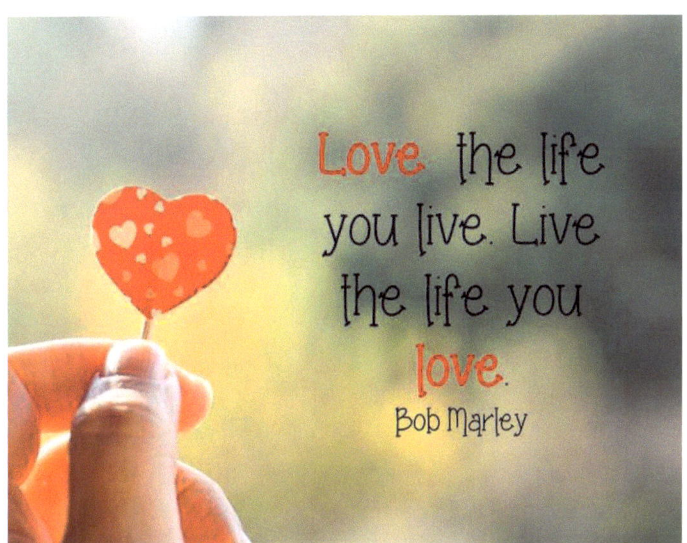